Private School Education in the U.S.

An Annotated Bibliography, 1950-1980

by
Alice H. Songe

Jefferson & London : McFarland
1982

206917

Library of Congress Cataloging in Publication Data

Songe, Alice H.
    Private school education in the U.S.

    Includes indexes.
    1. Private schools--United States--Bibliography.
I. Title.
Z5814. P65S58 [LC49]   016. 371'02'0973   81-20884
ISBN O-89950-045-5   AACR2

Manufactured in the United States of America

PREFACE

Ours is a nation in which education of the young has been termed a "public enterprise." Yet, private education was the only schooling provided for Americans from Colonial times until late in the 19th century, when the concept of publicly supported schools began to develop. As early as 1642, the Massachusetts Bay Colony made elementary education--then the "Three R's"--a parental responsibility which we, 400 hundred years later, call "family choice in education."

The role of the secular and church-related independent school is acknowledged to be one of tremendous importance in the life of our nation. Without the dual system of public and private schooling, the education of all American children would be an impossible task. Yet, the independent school, especially the church-related, has been, and continues to be a center of controversy, from the chambers of our national Congress to local governments and communities.

This bibliography is meant to provide sources of information representing all views of this controversy and to present the independent school as a justifiable and invaluable institution in a demcratic and pluralistic society.

TABLE OF CONTENTS

INTRODUCTION

The selective and annotated bibliography that follows these pages was designed to represent the body of literature published on nonpublic elementary and secondary education in the years 1950 through 1980, and to include several of the more important titles that appeared in 1981.

Generally, the scope of this work covers all aspects of the independent and church-related school--its aims and objectives, history, administration, financial, social and racial problems. More specifically, these sources seek to present recent and contemporary views on the controversies that seem to remain centered on nonpublic education. These controversial topics fall into four categories: (a) the constitutionality of providing public funds and services for church-related and other private schools; (b) the impact of such aid upon the public school system; (c) the rights of parents in choosing the type of schooling wanted for their children; (d) the elitist objectives of private schools versus the goals of a democratic society.

The items chosen are divided into four parts: books, monographs, serials; then Federal and state publications, followed by articles in periodicals and, lastly, doctoral dissertations.

Certain subject were intentionally not included in this listing. The first of these are the histories of individual schools and biographies of outstanding heads of such schools. Educators in private education who have contributed notable theories in education, such as Maria Montessori, and A. D. Neill, however, are included. Such histories and biographies are to be found listed in the excellent bibliography on nonpublic education compiled by Pauline Anderson (see item 114).

There was, also, an overwhelming number of periodical articles written on the pros and cons of public funds for Catholic parochial schools and the church-state question. Only a representative number of such sources are included in order to give balance. For those readers interested in these questions, the comprehensive bibliography by Brother Edmond Drouin (see item 33) is recommended.

        Selection was also of great importance when considering
the doctoral dissertations chosen for this study. As can be imagin-
ed, hundreds of such works on nonpublic education were produced in
the 30 year period covered by this bibliography. Those dissertations
preferred were limited to subjects of wide appeal and within the
scope mentioned in the beginning of this introduction.

        Another aspect that must be mentioned are the seemingly
insubstantial number of state publications on nonpublic education. Un
fortunately, such items, as a rule, are not listed in the more read-
ily available sources and proved difficult to locate.

        A feature of this book that will be useful to those organiz-
ing support for private education is the list of the national and state
associations concerned with nonpublic education at the elementary and
secondary level. For each association there is the latest information available on its address and the name of the chief executive of-
ficer.

        Ample subject and author indexes are also included in this
work. The author index, particularly, is of value in that it provides a name list of persons whose scholarly insights and opinions
have helped to shape private education in the last three decades.

        Finally it is hoped that this reference will prove useful not
only to those in the education community but to others such as state
and federal lawmakers concerned with legislation affecting private
schools, religious and lay persons responsible for church-related education, and social scientists and students engaged in the study of
American social life. Above all, the one group that may profit from
this list of information sources are the parents of school children,
responsible for their education, whether it be public or private. If
they choose the latter, this book will provide help in their decision.

        In the production of this book special thanks go to Eliza-
beth K. Porsche for editorial assistance, to Joanne Cassell of the
National Institute of Education Library, and to Judy Campbell of the
Educational Resources Information Center for valuable assistance in
research.

I. BOOKS, MONOGRAPHS, SERIALS

1. _AICS Compass_. 1946-. m. $9.00 Editor: Stephen B. Friedheim

   Journal of the Association of Independent Colleges and Schools. In addition to articles, the journal contains reviews of books related to independent school and college education.

2. _AMS Bulletin_. 1960-. q. Membership. Editor: Bretta Weiss

   Bulletin of the American Montessori Society. Contents centered mainly on the Montessori method of teaching, the administration of Montessori schools.

3. American Enterprise Institute for Public Policy Research. _Tuition Tax Credits and Alternatives_. Washington, D.C.: The Institute, 1978. 59p. (Legislative Analysis, 95th Congress, No. 27)

   This legislative analysis was made when a major struggle was taking place in Congress between supporters of proposals for tax credit for tuition payments to private educational institutions and supporters of President Carter's alternative proposals for building on to existing grant and loan programs. This report includes all of the pro and con arguments for this type of aid.

4. Baird, Leonard L. _The Elite Schools: A Profile of Prestigious Independent Schools_. Lexington, Mass.: Lexington Books, 1977. 156p.

   This study is based on information received from some 3,499 third and fourth year students and 1,000 teachers and administrators in 42 independent schools, mostly in the northeastern U.S. The book concentrates on the social and educational environment in which the students, teachers and administrators function and the type of culture the elite independent schools instill in their students.

5. Ban Joseph, D. _Education for Change_. Valley Forge, Pa.: The Judson Press, 1968. 126p.

   The author discusses Christian education as a change of lifestyle. He covers such areas as the objectives and philosophy of Christian education, the curriculum and the relationship of the private Christian school to public education.

6. Barrett, Joan, and Goldfarb, Sally F. _The Insiders' Guide to Prep Schools_. New York: E.P. Dutton, 1979. 232p.

Written by former "preppies" (now staff members of the Yale Daily News), this book gives advice to young people who are planning to enter independent schools. A general commentary is included, along with statistics and facts about 69 boarding schools throughout the U.S.

7. Becker, Henry J. The Impact of Racial Composition and Public School Desegregation on Changes in Non-Public School Enrollment by White Pupils. Baltimore: Johns Hopkins University, Center for Social Organization of Schools, 1978. 38p. (Report No. 252.)

The research was sponsored by the U.S. National Institute of Education. It describes the changes between 1960 and 1970 of private school enrollments and how these changes are associated with the shifts in the cities' demographic racial makeup.

8. Bennett, Hal. No More Public School. New York: Random House, 1972. 138p.

This book is intended primarily for parents and is a "how-to" guide for taking a child out of public school and starting a private school for his education. It contains information on such essentials as equipment, legal incorporation, administration and staff. The author also provides advice as to how to get the child back into public school, should the private venture fail.

9. Blackmer, A.R. An Inquiry into Student Unrest in Independent Schools. Boston: National Association of Independent Schools, 1970. 80 p.

A brief survey of the causes of student unrest in the late 1960's. Useful as a study for student life at that period.

10. Blanshard, Paul. Religion in the Schools: The Great Controversy. Boston: Beacon Press, 1963. 244p.

A well researched and documented study of all of the controversies related to church and state in American education, from the presidency of Thomas Jefferson to that of John F. Kennedy. The Rev. Robert F. Drinan, S;J., presents views opposing that of the author regarding parochial school education.

11. Blum, Virgil C. Freedom in Education: Federal Aid for All Children. Garden City, N.Y.: Doubleday, 1965. 235p.

The author uses numerous Supreme Court decisions to advocate that parents have a right to a free choice in the education of their children, but that right is violated when public funds are denied to provate schools.

12.   Bogardus, LaDonna. Christian Education for Retarded Persons. New York: Abingdon Press, 1969. 112p.
Treatment of an unusual approach to privately educating mentally retarded students. Besides describing special education programs, the author includes information on instructional materials, teaching methods and religious instruction.

13.   Bower, William C., and Hayward, Percy R. Protestantism Faces Its Educational Task Together. Appleton, Wis.: C.C. Nelson, 1950. 292p.
A survey of Protestant education at midcentury. Includes a discussion of the organizational structure of Protestant schools, the environmental influences upon it and the research done in this field.

14.   Brickman, William W. Educational Systems in the United States. New York: Center for Applied Research in Education, 1964. 118p.
The history of education in the U.S. is a history of both private and public education. With the dual system in mind, Brickman describes the organization of both, controversies in which private education is involved, church-state relations and racially segregated schools.

15.   Brinton, Howard H. Quaker Education in Theory and Practice. Wallingford, Pa.: Pendle Hill Pamphlets, 1958. 111p.
A brief history of Quaker education and a look forward in regard to objectives and policies.

16.   Burton, Alma P. Karl G. Maeser, Mormon Educator. Salt Lake City: Deseret Book Co., 1953. 79p.
Besides providing biographical information on Karl G. Maeser, this monograph presents the Mormon philosophy of education and facts concerning the Brigham Young Academy.

17.   Butler, Henry E., Jr. "Legal Basis of State Relations to Nonpublic Schools." In Encyclopedia of Education, Vol. 8, edited by Lee C. Deighton (New York: Macmillan and the Free Press, 1971), p. 442-7.
This article covers the Supreme Court decisions related to the regulation of nonpublic schools, textbooks and transportation, shared time, dual enrollments and indirect payments from public funds.

18.   CAPE Outlook. May 1974-. 10/yr. $7.00 Editor: Carla Gelband.

Previously published as Outlook, this official publication of the Council for American Private Education contains brief articles on nonpublic education in various states. Of special interest is the regular column "Washington" which serves as an up-date on federal legislation and activities related to private education.

19. Cadwallader, E. M. A History of Seventh-Day Adventist Education. Lincoln, Neb.: Union College, 1958. 314p.
A good source for the historical beginnings of Seventh-Day Adventist education in the U.S. Includes information on the Battle Creek School and Bell's Schools.

20. Cass, James. "Church, State and School" In Education in America, 1960-1969; The Educational Supplement of the Saturday Review in Four Volumes (New York: Arno Press, 1960-). Vol. I, p. 260-261; 270-71.
An analysis of the then current debate on the constitutionality of Federal government aid to Catholic Schools, and the implications for the separation of church and state in our society. Cass offers a "possible course of action" to be taken should the Supreme Court declare such aid as constitutional.

21. Christian Home and School. 10/yr. $3.25 Editor: Kenneth Swets.
Journal of the National Union of Christian Schools and available only through the Union. Contains articles and book reviews of interest to Christian parents and educators.

22. Christian Teacher. 1963-. bi-m. (except July and August). $5.00. Editor: Herman E. van Schuyver.
Official journal of the National Association of Christian Schools. The articles and book reviews are indexed in the Christian Periodical Index.

23. The Church's Schools in a Changing World: Proceedings of the Washington Conference, November 3-5, 1960. Edited by Clarence W. Brickman. Greenwich, Conn.: Seabury Press, 1961. 80p.
Participants Stephen F. Bayne, Jr., Clarence W. Brickman, David R. Hunter, Arthur Lichtenberger and F. Edward Lund contributed papers on the curriculum of the church school, its relationship to the parish church and modern philosophies affecting church-related education, such as existentialism.

24. Cogdell, Gaston D. What Price Parochiaid? A Comprehensive Analysis of the Reasons Why Public Funds Should Not Be Used for Nonpublic Schools. Silver Spring, Md.: Americans United for Separation of Church and State, 1970. 271p.

The author believes that "parochiaid" (i. e. aid to church-related schools) is not wanted or needed, and that it will undermine democracy and create a "de facto" establishment of religion. Most of Cogdell's criticism is directed at Catholic schools.

25.   Cohen, Jack J. Jewish Education in a Democratic Society. New York: Reconstructionist Press, 1964. 350 p.
A review of some of the finer points of Jewish education such as indoctrination vs. education, communal cooperation in providing Jewish schools, the effects of leisure time on the schools' programs.

26.   Cooley, Charles A. Fund-Raising for the Private School: The Foundation Approach. Cambridge, Mass.: Crimson Printing Co., 1968. 159p.
A review of the sources available for aid to private schools such as government aid, fund-raising of various kinds, with emphasis on getting support from philanthropic foundations.

27.   Coons, John E., and Sugarman, Stephen D. Education by Choice: The Case for Family Control. Berkeley: University of California Press, 1979. 249p.
An examination of the philosophical and pragmatic issues involved when a family chooses it own form of schooling for its children. Alternative plans and aids are suggested, such as the voucher system. An appendix, "Introducing Family Choice in Education Through State Constitutional Change" is also a valuable source of information for families considering alternative schooling.

28.   Cumerford, William R. Fund Raising--A Professional Guide. Fort Lauderdale, Fla.: School World, 1980. 347p.
The author, a professional fund raiser, provides a useful reference for the headmaster and others responsible for raising funds for private schools.

29.   Curran, Francis X. The Churches and the Schools: American Protestantism and Popular Elementary Education. Chicago: Loyola University Press, 1954. 152p.
A summary and historical background of the elementary education system provided by these mainline Protestant churches: Baptists, Congregationalists, Episcopalians, Methodists and Quakers. A bibliography is also included.

30.   Dahlberg, Henry Jr. Analytical Study of Instructional Personnel Policies in NAIS Member Schools. Boston: National Association of Independent Schools, 1972. 24p.
The results of a poll taken of 721 private schools that yielded a response rate of 84 percent. The resulting data is broken down into five categories: boarding schools, day schools, enrollments, salary ranges and geographic locations.

31. Davenport, Stephen. "Farewell to the Old School Tie." In
Education in America, 1960-1969: The Educational Supplement of
the Saturday Review in Four Volumes (New York: Arno Press,
1960-), Vol. 4, p. 524-7, 538.
    A summary of integration in private secondary schools and
the problems involved in breaking down existing racial barriers. The
author maintains that the problems run deeper than mere "superficial
social relationships."

32. Dodds, Harold W. "Your Youngster and the Public School."
In The Public Schools in Crisis; Some Critical Essays. Edited by
Mortimer Smith (Chicago: H. Regnery, 1956), p. 63-70.
    A design to help parents to evaluate and choose a private
school, should they find public schooling inadequate.

33. Drouin, Edmond G. (Brother). The School Question: A
Bibliography on Church-State Relationships in American Education,
1940-1960. Washington, D.C.: Catholic University of America Press,
1963. 261p.
    A comprehensive bibliography of over 1,399 entries that cover
every aspect of church-state relationships for the period studied.
Emphasis is on the controversies surrounding public aid for Catholic
parochial schools.

34. Dubay, Thomas. Philosophy of the State as Educator. Milwaukee, Wis.: Bruce Pub. Co., 1959. 237p.
    An examination of the legal role of the state in education.
Chapters are devoted to such topics as "the Catholic position" in
education, and how the modern state must assist private initiative in
education by providing needed financial assistance.

35. Educational Freedom and the Case for Government Aid to
Students in Independent Schools. Edited by Daniel D. McGarry and
Leo Ward. Milwaukee, Wis.: Bruce Pub. Co., 1966. 226p.
    This book is a collaborative enterprise of 15 contributors.
Although varying in faiths and opinions, all agree that students in
independent schools should not be excluded from sharing in educational tax funds. A selected bibliography on public aid to nonpublic schoo
by Brother Edmond G. Drouin is included.

36. Educational Vouchers: Concepts and Controversies. Edited
by George R. LaNoue. New York: Teachers College, Columbia Univ
ersity, 1972. 176p.
    Professionals, such as religious leaders, politicans, lawyers,
judges, economists and philosophers contributed their ideas for and
against the use of educational vouchers. Related questions such as
racial integration, parochial school aid, equitable tax policies are
given full treatment.

37. The Episcopal Church and Education. Edited by Kendig B.
Cully. New York: Morehouse-Barlow Co., 1966. 256p.
     Editor Cully and 14 other contributors present a status re-
port on the school system sponsored by the Episcopal Church. In
the discussions an historical perspective and words on administration
are also given.

38. Erickson, Donald A. Philanthropy, Public Needs, and Nonpublic Schools. A Report. Washington, D.C.: Council for American
Private Education, 1974. 57p.
     This report discusses the effects of philanthropy on nonpublic
elementary and secondary schools, causing them to be more financially efficient, more effective in educational performance and more
humane in impact upon parents and students.

39. _____ . "Public Funds for Private Schools." In Education
in America, 1960-1969; The Educational Supplement of The Saturday
Review in Four Volumes (New York: Arno Press, 1960-), Vol. 4,
p. 592-04, 514-15.
     Erickson details his ideas on the advantages to be gained in
giving public funds for private school education. He cites the inadeq-
uacy of the public school system in meeting all of the educational
needs of our youth and suggests vouchers and tuition tax credits as
a means of giving public support to maintain private schools.

40. _____ , and Greeley, Andrew M. "Nonpublic Schools and
Metropolitanism." In Yearbook of the National Society for the Study
of Education, 1968: Metropolitanism--Its Challenge to Education,
edited by Robert J. Havighurst (Chicago: University of Chicago Press,
1968), p. 287-98.
     The authors discuss the impact of nonpublic schools on public
school enrollments, divisiness caused by certain types of private
schooling, academic quality and competition for moral and financial
support. Numerous studies are documented to support their theories
and views.

41. Esty, John C., Jr. Choosing a Private School. New York:
Dodd, Mead, 1974. 267p.
     Written primarily for parents, this book examines the nature
and characteristics of the ideal in private school education. Esty
furnishes insights as to "why this country needs its private school
system as an alternative to the public school monopoly."

42. Fantini, Mario D. Public Schools of Choice. New York:
Simon & Schuster, 1973. 256p.

     Fantini presents a scheme for educational reform whereby
public school students would be given a wide choice of schooling in

nonpublic institutions. He believes that such freedom of choice is necessary if our diverse population is to be sufficiently educated, without depending entirely on the monolithic public school system.

43.   Federal Aid and Catholic Schools.   Edited by Daniel Callahan. Baltimore: Helicon Pub. Co. , 1964.   160p.
Ten brief essays on the question of federal aid to Catholic schools are contributed by scholars of various faiths.   The opinions given represent public educational policy and attitudes on public funds for Catholic and other church-related schools.

44.   Fichter, Joseph H. Parochial School: A Sociological Study. Notre Dame, Ind.: University of Notre Dame Press, 1958.   495p.
A clear, unbiased report centered mainly on parochial elementary school education.   Such topics as family influences, finances, parent-teacher relationships, pluralism and tuition are covered.

45.   Fourth Annual Conference on Public and Non-Public Schools: Value Education. December 1, 1977. Proceedings.   Edited by Seymour P. Lachman. New York: City University of New York, Center for Advanced Study in Education, 1978.   69p.
This conference was convened to offer a forum for the discussion of value education, as moral dilemmas related to educational trends and the moral development of students.   Dr. Edwin Fenton of the Carnegie-Mellon Education Center gave the keynote address.

46.   Friedlander, Anna F. The Shared Time Strategy: Prospects and Trends in the Growing Partnership Between Public and Church Schools. St Louis: Concordia Pub. Co. , 1960.   87p.
A short but informative monograph on the constitutional implications of shared time between parochial and public schools.   Contains a comprehensive bibliography on the subject.

47.   Fuess, Claude M. "Golden Days for Independent Schools." Education in America, 1960-1969; The Educational Supplement of the Saturday Review in Four Volumes (New York: Arno Press, 1960-), Vol. I, p. 588-90, 695
The headmaster emeritus of Phillips Andover writes of the accomplishments of private education and of the leadership displayed in achieving these goals.   He also presents the criticism levelled at the private schools from various segments of our society

48.   _____ . Independent School Masters. Boston: Little, Brown 1952. 371p.
Views on what the ideal headmaster of a private school should be, particularly in the fields of administration and of human relationships.

49.   Gaines, Richard L.   The Finest Education Money Can Buy: A Concerned Look at America's Prestige Schools.   New York: Simon & Schuster, 1972.   255p.

A first-person narrative study of the values, objectives and day-to-day activites of the American private school as seen in a comparative study of two of the most expensive and exclusive-- Lawrenceville School (N. J.) and Newton South (Mass.).   Because of the author's longer association with Lawrenceville, the emphasis of his writing is centered upon it.

50.   General Education in School and College: A Committee Report by Members of the Faculties of Andover,   Exeter, Lawrenceville, Harvard, Princeton and Yale.   Cambridge, Mass.:   Harvard University Press, 1952.   142p.

A research report on the relationships of the last two years of preparatory school and the first two years in college.   Useful as a review of the transition from private school to college, what the expectations are, what is actually realized.

51.   Giannella, Donald A.   "Private Schools, State Supervision of."   In New Catholic Encyclopedia, Vol. 11 (New York: McGraw-Hill, 1967), p.   895-07

This article presents the constitutional limits over the states in their exercise of the supervision and regulation of private schools. The statutory provisions of the states in such areas as curriculum, teachers, buildings, admissions and expulsions are also discussed.

52.   Giles, Michael W. , and others.   Desegration and The Private School Alternative.   Washington, D. C.: Catholic University of America, Center for National Policy Review, 1975.   11p.

A summary report of research sponsored by the National Institute of Education.   The study was an intensive survey of seven desegregated school districts in Florida and gives the opinions of the parents in these districts, who decided to send their children to private segregated schools.

53.   Government Aid to Nonpublic Schools: Yes or No?   Edited by George A. Kelly.   New York: St. John's Press, 1972.   99p.

Nine contributors, including such persons as Donald Barr, New York Governor Hugh L. Carey and Seymour Lachiman, discuss the legal implications of public aid for private schools, pluralism in American society and the public benefits to be had from private education.

54.   Graubord, Allen.   Free the Children: Radical Reform and the Free School Movement.   New York: Pantheon Books, 1972. 306p.

The author, a former MIT philosophy professor, spent three years as a participant observer of "free schools."   The major part of the book describes the scope and character of these schools, how and why they came into existence, and the problems they face as experimental alternative systems of education.

55. Greeley, Andrew M. and Rossi, Peter H. The Education of Catholic Americans. Chicago: Aldine Publishing Co., 1966. 250p.
    A study funded by the Carnegie Corporation and the former U.S. Department of Health, Education and Welfare, to determine the social effects of Catholic parochial school education. The research is on the consequences of Catholic education between 1910 and 1960.

56. A Handbook for Independent School Operation. Edited by William Johnson. Princeton, N.J.: Van Nostrand, 1961. 296p.
    A group of 12 educators express their views on the operation of successful independent schools and cover such topics as finance, curriculum, and public relations. An extensive chapter on boarding is included.

57. Heeley, Allan V. "Private Schools in American Education." In Public Education in America, edited by G.A. Bereday and L. Volpicelli, (New York: Harper & Row, 1958), p. 50-61
    Heeley defines the place that private schools hold in our American democracy and the proper education of a superior minority. He presents the limitations under which American private schools must operate.

58. _____. Why the Private School. New York: Harper, 1951. 208p.
    This book is divided into two parts. The first deals with the place of the private school in our society and the second part discusses the programs of these institutions. Although now a bit outdated, the information presented will prove useful to parents who are planning on private education for their children.

59. Holt, John. Teach Your Own: A Hopeful Path for Education. New York: Delacorte, 1981. 369p.
    Parents who have decided to remove their children from school and to teach them at home will find this book helpful. The author supplies the arguments for their choice and gives information to defend their choice, even in court.

60. ISACS Bulletin. 1963-. s-a. $3.00. Editor: Robert Matson.
    This official journal of the Independent School Association of the Central States appears but twice a year. In addition to articles, the bulletin offers reviews of books related to independent education.

61. Illich, Ivan. Deschooling Society. New York: Harper & Row, 1971. 116p.
    When first published, this book was considered a "revolutionary document", as the author stated that the present public school

system is "obsolete" and that the education of our children must be done in other ways, including private education. Illich's ideas will have great appeal for those interested in alternative schooling, and how this form of education may be realized.

62. Independent School. 1941-. q. $10.00.   Editor: Blair McElroy.
The official journal of the National Association of Independent Schools, formerly called the Independent School Bulletin. Contains a feature articles, the NAIS Reporter, special news of NAIS members and book reviews.

63. Independent School Commentary Panel. The Expanding School Environment: A Response by the Independent School Commentary Panel to Recent Studies of Secondary Education.   Boston: Commission on Educational Issues (NAIS), 1978. 165p.
The Panel, made up of six experienced private school heads debated such issues as isolation of the private school, "dejuvenilization" of the secondary school, the organization of change.

64. Kemerer, Frank R.   Understanding Faculty Unions and Collective Bargaining. Boston: National Association of Independent Schools, 1976. 69p.
This monograph may be described as a guide for administrators to help them understand working conditions that call for unionization among faculty members. An appendix outlines a sample personnel policy and a glossary defines labor terms.

65. Kozol, Jonathan. Free Schools. Boston: Houghton Mifflin Company, 1972. 146p.
A handbook written from the author's long experience with the free school movement. Although the style may be questionable by some, because of the occasional use of indecent language, the information on how to start and maintain a free school is complete and professional.

66. Kraushaar, Otto F. American Nonpublic Schools: Patterns of Diversity. Baltimore, Md., and London, Eng.: The Johns Hopkins University Press, 1972. 387p.
A well documented study that includes an historical review of nonpublic education in America, a nationwide survey of school constituencies, the changing role of private education, and a discussion of public issues relating to private schools. Contains copious footnotes, but lacks a bibliography of sources mentioned.

67. _____ . Private Schools: From the Puritans to the Present. Bloomington, Ind.: Phi Delta Kappa, 1976. 55p. (Fastback Series No. 78, Bicentennial Series)
A concise review of the history of church-related and independent schools, from Colonial times until the late 19th century.

Kraushaar believes that both public and private schools must work together to overcome the problems that result from their frequently uneasy partnership.

68.   Larson, Martin A.   When Parochial Schools Close: A Study in Educational Financing. Washington, D.C.: R. B. Luce, 1972. 312p.
      Parochial school systems in 12 states are reviewed here, including schools of the Missouri Synod (Lutheran), the Mormon Churcl and Seventh-Day Adventists congregations.   The effects of the federal Elementary and Secondary Education Act of 1965 upon parochial schools is also discussed.

69.   Leib, Robert J. U.S. Private Schools Classified.   Los Angeles: Sherbourne Press, 1968-.
      Schools are classified into mainly independent, church-related, college preparatory and military schools.   Information includes school location by state, admission policies, whether co-ed or not.

79.   Lerner, Barbara.   Minimum Competence, Maximum Choice: Second Chance Legislation.   New York: Irvington Publishers, Inc., 1980. 200p.
      An innovative idea concerning educational vouchers.   Lerner believes that all students in public schools should be given minimum competency tests, and that those who cannot achieve academically for a 3-year period should be given educational vouchers for transfer to a private school, also for a trial period.   If the student does not improve after 3 years the private school should not be allowed to keep him at state expense.

71.   Locigno, Joseph P.   Education: To Whom Does It Belong? New York: Desclee Company, Inc., 1968. 184p.
      A view of shared time education from the Catholic position. The author believes that shared time is one way of allowing church and state to jointly educate children.   Has a bibliography.

72.   Love, Robert.   How to Start Your Own School: A Guide for the Radical Right, the Radical Left and Everybody in-Between Who Is Fed Up with Public Education. New York: Macmillan Co., 1973. 172p.
      As the title indicates this is a "how-to" guide for would-be organizers of an alternative school system.   Advice is given on such important items as accreditation, certification, boards of trustees, libraries and tuition charges.

73.   Luebke, Paul T.   American Elementary and Secondary Community Schools Abroad.   2nd ed. Arlington, Va.: American Association of School Administrators, 1975. 51p.

A description and assessment of the schools that are support-ed in part by grants-in-aid from the U.S. State Department, and are attended by children whose parents live abroad.

74.   Lynes, David, and Opdycke, Leonard E. Notes on Trusteeship. Boston: National Association of Independent Schools, 1875. 23p.
     Although brief this paper deals with an important aspect of private school administration--the relationship of the school's auth-orities with that of the corporation and board of trustees.

75.   McLachlan, James. America's Boarding Schools: A Histor-ical Study. New York: Scribner's, 1970. 381p.
     In this study the author stresses the fact that the American boarding school is uniquely American and not a British importation. He traces the history of the boarding school from Colonial times to the post-progressive period. The book also contains comments on many schools and biographical information on notable private school educators.

76.   McMillan, William J. Private School Management. Second edition. Fort Lauderdale, Fla.: Ferguson E. Peters, Co., 1979. 188p.
     A professional source for private school management, especi-ally the financial aspects. Topics include budgeting, insurance pro-grams, fringe benefits for faculty, retirement plans.

77.   _____. Private Schools: Boards and Heads. Fort Laud-erdale, Fla.: Ferguson E. Peters, Co., 1980. 88p.
     A guide designed for those engaged in administering to day and boarding schools. Innovative ideas for a successful school are also presented by the author, himself a headmaster of achievement.

78.   Mallery, David. Negro Students in Independent Schools. Boston: National Association of Independent Schools, 1963. 93p.
     In this brief monograph, the relationship between black and white students is dicussed as well as the morale of black students in independent schools.

79.   _____. New Approaches in Education: A Study of Experi-mental Programs in Independent Schools. Boston: National Council of Independent Schools, 1961. 182p.
     A review of some of the newer programs possible in inde-pendent schools including apprenticeships, intercultural education, international studies, interracial learning situations.

80.   Manning, Leonard F. "Private School Pupils, Free textbooks for". In New Catholic Encyclopedia. Vol. 11. New York: McGraw-Hill, 1967. p. 693-95.

An overview of enacted Federal and State laws providing free textbooks for private school children and brief discussions of the cases that brought these rulings into existence.

81.   Meranto, Philip.   The Politics of Federal Aid to Education in 1965: A Study in Political Innovation.   Syracuse, N.Y.:   Syracuse University Press, 1967.   144p.
An in-depth case study of the Elementary and Secondary Education Act of 1965 and its provisions for private schools.

82.   Miller, Arthur S.   Racial Discrimination and Private Education: A Legal Analysis.   Chapel Hill, N.C.:   University of North Carolina Press, 1957.   136p.
The legal problems involved in the racial desegregation of church-related and other private schools.   The introductory chapter "The Private School System in America" provides the legal basis for other dicussions on governmental sanction against integration and the public nature of private schooling.

83.   Miller, Marilyn F., and Duvall, Charles R.   An Annotated Bibliography of Literature Dealing With the Issues of Sectarian Schoc and Vouchering.   South Bend, Ind.:   Indiana University, 1979.   22p.
The citations given are from periodicals, and New York Times articles, editorials, letters and advertisements.   Besides the subject of vouchers, such subjects as government and school relationships, tax credits, and the effects of government aid on private elementary school education are included.

84.   Momentum.   1970-.   4/yr. $10.00 Editor: Carl Balcerals.
Official journal of the National Catholic Education Association Besides articles the journal contains book reviews and bibliographies Indexed in leading national indexes.

85.   Montessori and the Special Child.   Edited by R.C. Orem.   Ne York: G.P. Putnam's Sons, 1969.   232p.
Essays by 14 contributors on the possibilities of using the Montessori method of teaching in order to educate the handicapped child.   Cybernetic and sensorimotor approaches are discussed as we as the role of educational technology.

86.   Moynihan, Daniel P.   Government and the Ruin of Private Education.   New York: Harper and Row, 1978.   256p.
Senator Moynihan contends that tax credits for tuition provide a way by which nonpublic schools can be supported.   He also review the origins of public education, the Supreme Court rulings that exclu private schools and pluralism in American Society.

87. Muse, Benjamin. Virginia's Massive Resistance. Bloomington, Ind.: Indiana University Press, 1961. 184p.
    Useful as an example of how a Southern state organized to
prevent desegregation of its private schools. Includes information
on the "Gray Plan", tuition grants and vouchers.

88. National Association of Independent Schools. Accounting for
Independent Schools. Second edition. Boston: The Association, 1977.
205 p.
    Guidelines to the best current accounting, reporting, manage-
ment and planning practices are offered in this revised edition of a
work first published in 1969.

89. _____. Ad Hoc Library Committee. Books for Secondary
School Libraries. . . . Sixth edition. New York: R. R. Bowker,
1981. 844p.
    A recommended list of "best books" suitable in establishing
and maintaining a library in a public as well as private secondary
school.

90. _____. Commission on Educational Issues. Survey of Public Interest and Other Innovative Programs. Boston: The Association, 1977. 84p.
    A directory of information on innovative programs in the pri-
vate schools affiliated with NAIS.

91. National Conference on Private Educational Research, November 29 - December 2, 1977. Proceedings. Washington, D.C.:
Council for American Private Education, 1978. 26, 15p. (Type-
script.)
    A summary of papers presented by such authorities on pri-
vate education as Donald A. Erickson, William C. McCready and
Frank B. Brouillet. The conference was sponsored by the U.S. National Institute of Education.

92. Nevins, David, and Bills, Robert E. The Schools That Fear
Built. Washington, D.C.: Acropolis Books, 1976. 186p.
    Each author contributes a part of this two-part book on the
schools or "segregated academies" established in the South in the
wake of integregation orders from the Supreme Court. Nevin's report is a qualitative survey on the nature of these schools, and
Bills discusses 11 particular schools in existence.

93. Newton, Willoughby. "Protestant Parochial Schools." In
Education in America, 1960-1969; The Educational Supplement of
the Saturday Review in Four Volumes (New York: Arno Press, 1960-)
vol. I, p. 616-7.

The author points out the fact that for many people the term "parochial school" refers to the Catholic school system only. He raises important questions as to the organization and quality of Protestant parochial schools.

94. Nonpublic Aid: The Law, Economics and Politics of American Education. Edited by E.G. West. Lexington, Mass.: Lexington Books, 1975. 158p.

This work considers the role that government should and could play in financially helping private schools. The main contents consist of eight essays on this subject. E.G. West writes a response to easy essay, thus giving the reader a wide choice of pro and con opinions on nonpublic school aid.

95. "The Nonpublic Schools". In America's Educational Tradition An Interpretive History. By William M. French, Boston, Mass.: D. C. Heath and Company, 1964. p. 275-94.

A brief history of the rise of private schools, under the auspices of multiple religious groups. Other subjects such as federal aid to church-related schools and Supreme court decisions affecting private education are also treated.

96. "The Nonpublic Schools". In Financing the Schools: What Should be the Policy Toward Financing Elementary and Secondary Education in the United States? Washington, D.C.: American Enterprise Institute for Public Policy Research, 1972. p. 35-41.

The main work is an analysis of the 1972-1973 debate topic. The chapter on nonpublic schools deals with its role in our society. all aspects of public funds for private education, alternative aid proposals as tuition tax credits and other benefits.

97. On Equality of Educational Opportunity. Edited by Frederick Mosteller and Daniel Moynihan. New York: Random House, 1972. 570 p.

This book contains the papers resulting from the Harvard University faculty seminar on the report by James S. Coleman entitled On Equality of Education Opportunity. The seminar, held during the 1966-67 academic year, covers those aspects of private schooling covered in the Coleman report.

98. O'Toole, Thomas J. "Private School Pupils, Public Transportation for". In New Catholic Encyclopedia, vol. 11 (New York: McGraw-Hill, 1967). p. 797-300.

Federal and state laws providing bus transportation for parochial school children are reviewed, with individual court cases cited. Also traeated is the status of church-state relations in the United States.

99.   Parkman, Francis, and Springer, E. Laurence. <u>The Independent School Trustee Handbook.</u>   Boston: National Association of Independent Schools, 1974.   66p.   Third edition.
     Designed mainly for trustees of private schools, this handbook will be found useful by those who serve on boards of various types, in and out of the field of education.   New material added to this edition covers the orientation of new trustees and guidelines to be used in evaluating the performance of both the school and its headmaster.

100.   <u>Planning for Lutheran High Schools.</u>   St. Louis, Mo.: Lutheran Church, Missouri Synod; Milwaukee, Wis.: Wisconsin Evangelical Lutheran Synod, 1978-.
     A series of seven handbooks designed to help Lutheran community leaders to organize and maintain schools.   Information includes financial planning, transportation, school management.

101.   Polking, Joseph C.   "Private School Pupils, Health and Welfare Services for".   In <u>New Catholic Encyclopedia,</u> vol. 11 (New York: McGraw-Hill, 1967), p. 795-97.
     The legislative provisions of state and federal governments covering the health, safety and school lunch programs of private school children.   The author also presents the Constitutional justification for such benefits.

102.   Powell, Theodore.   <u>The School Bus Law: A Case Study in Education, Religion and Politics.</u> Middletown, Conn.: Wesleyan University Press, 1960.   334p.
     An overview of the national and state of Connecticut legislation affecting church-related schools.   A detailed analysis of the 1957 Connecticut law providng bus transportation at public expense is also presented.

103.   "Private Education" In <u>Law in the Schools.</u> By William D. Valente (Columbus, Ohio: Charles E. Merrill, 1980), p. 453-523.
     Seven aspects of law related to private education are discussed in this chapter.   These include such areas as teacher status and rights, antidiscrimination, government financial assistance, state regulation of private education.   Particular cases are cited in the footnotes.

104.   <u>Private School Newsletter.</u> 1970-. 9/yr. $27.00.   Edited by the publishing staff of School World, Fort Lauderdale, Fla.
     Abstracts of important reports, including governmental reports and news articles of interest to educators and parents.

105. "Public Aid to Parochial Schools." In Federal Aid to Education, edited by Ronald Steel (New York: H.W. Wilson Co., 1961), p. 95-137 (The Reference Shelf, vol. 33).

A collection of articles on the 1961-62 high school debate topic. This chapter gives all arguments for and against federal aid to Catholic parochial schools.

106. Public Controls for Nonpublic Schools. Edited by Donald A. Erickson. Chicago: University of Chicago Press, 1969. 242p.

Ten papers given at the national invitational conference on "State Regulation of Nonpublic Schools", sponsored by the Midwest Administration Center, University of Chicago, March 28 and 29, 1967. Besides discussing state regulations of private schools, the papers included the Amish controversy in Iowa, racial discrimination in private schools and the "Catholic viewpoint" on state regulation and parochial schools.

107. Radical School Reform. Edited by Beatrice Gross and Ronald Gross. New York: Simon and Schuster, 1969. 350p.

Twenty-four contributors, including such educators as Sylvia Ashton-Warner, John Holt, Jonathan Kozol, Kenneth Clark and Herbert Kohl furnish scholarly opinions on alternative methods of schooling, problems in public education that call for school reform, community schools and special education programs.

108. Religious Education: A Comprehensive Survey. Edited by Marvin J. Taylor. New York: Abingdon Press, 1960. 446p.

An exhaustive review of the status and function of the church-related schools by 49 contributors. All aspects of Catholic, Jewish and Protestant schools are presented.

109. Ritter, Paul M. The Business Manager in the Independent School. Boston, Mass.: National Association of Independent Schools, 1979. 49p.

This monograph is a revised one from the 1967 edition. It up-dates and re-defines the position of the business manager, the training, background and experience most needed for successful management in the independent school.

110. The Role of the Independent Schools in American Democracy Papers delivered at a Conference on Education ... May 8, 9 and 10 1956. Milwaukee, Wis.: Marquette University Press, 1956. 146p.

The conference was held to mark the anniversary celebration of Marquette. Twelve papers by outstanding educators were given, dealing mostly with justification for private schooling, the constitutional implications for it, relationship to public schools.

111. Sargent, Porter. Directory for Exceptional Children, 1981-82. 9th edition. Boston: Porter Sargent Publishers, Inc., 1981. 1384p.

A listing of over 3,000 schools, facilities, and organizations in the United States concerned with handicapped children. Both public and private facilities are covered, including boarding schools, outpatient clinics, residential and day facilities.

112. _____. Handbook of Private Schools. 61st edition. Boston: Porter Sargent Publishers, Inc., 1980. 1448p.

Current facts and school histories on 1800 elementary and secondary boarding and day schools. "Private Schools Illustrated" is a distinctive feature within the book, containing 500 photographs of facilities and grounds of some of the schools.

113. _____. Schools Abroad of Interest to Americans. Boston: Porter Sargent Publishers, Inc., 1979. 464p.

A description of over 900 elementary and secondary schools in 125 countries. Diplomatic and corporate personnel will also find this a useful source.

114. A Selected Bibliography of Literature on the Independent School. Compiled by Pauline Anderson. Milton, Mass.: Independent Schools Education Board, 1959. 120p.

A comprehensive bibliography with the time span going back to the 19th century. The arrangement, however, detracts from the book as the subject, author and title entries are in one alphabet, causing titles to be repeated several times over. An excellent source for the histories of individual schools and for biographical information on headmasters and headmistresses.

115. Sizer, Theodore R. The Age of the Academies. New York: Teachers College, Columbia University, 1964. 201.

An historical review of early American academies, the attitudes of colonial Americans toward them, the subjects taught. The opinions of Benjamin Franklin on education are also discussed.

116. Spurlock, Clark. Education and the Supreme Court. Urbana: University of Illinois Press, 1955. 252p.

A specialized study of the 45 cases in which the Supreme Court issued decisions affecting education, public and nonpublic.

117. Spykman, Gordon, and others. Society, State and Schools: A Case for Structural and Confessional Pluralism. Grand Rapids, Mich.: William B. Eerdmans, 1981. 225p.

Public funding of nonpublic schools has long been a center of controversy in American life. This study, produced by the Fellows of the Calvin Center for Christian Scholarship introduces a new aspec of this debate by providing evangelical theories as an argument for public aid to private education.

118.   State and Federal Laws Relating to Nonpublic Schools. Compiled by Helen M. Jessison.   Silver Spring, Md.:   Bascombe Associates, Inc.   1975.   366p.
Compilation of constitutional and statutory provisions affecting nonpublic elementary and secondary schools and the children who attend them.   Five introductory chapters give information as the current status of nonpublic schools, the effect of federal laws on state responsibilities for private education.

119.   Stellhorn, August C.   Schools of the Lutheran Church-Missour Synod.   St. Louis, Mo.:   Concordia Publishing House, 1963.   507p.
A perspective on Lutheran education that includes a discussion upon legislation affecting the school system, teacher training pr grams and the text books used in the schools.

120.   Strong, Dexter K.   Handbook for New Heads: An Introduction to Independent School Administration.   Boston: National Association for Independent Schools, 1977.   76p.
Guidance for those committed to heading an independent school.   All hazards, demands and responsibilities of the position are presented in detail.

121.   Summerhill: For and Against. New York: Hart Publishing Co., Inc., 1970.   271p.
Fifteen prominent educators and other scholars such as Bruno Bettelheim, Erich Fromm, and Paul Goodman present arguments for and against the educational and disciplinary methods of the experimental educator A.S. Neill, founder of the Summerhill school.

122.   Swanson, Austin D., and Igoe, Joseph A.   Should Public Monies be Used to Support Nonpublic Education? A Review of the Issues and Practices.   Danville, Ill.:   Interstate Printers and Publishers, Inc., 1967.   71p.
The four chapters in this monograph deal with the historical and legal developments of public monies for private schools, the philosophical issues involved, the status (in 1967) of existing public assistance programs and a comparative survey of public support for nonpublic schools in other nations.

123.   Swomley, John M., Jr.   Religion, the State and the Schools.
New York: Pegasus, 1968.   220p.
   A summary of religious and secular views in regard to
church-state relationships in public and private schooling, with emphasis on the Elementary and Secondary Education Act of 1965.

124.   Tucker, Gilbert M.   The Private School: Its Advantages,
Its Problems, Its Finances. New York: Vantage Press, 1965.   127
p.
   Covers a wide range of subjects related to private schooling.   The author also writes of academic freedom, federal aid to
nonpublic schools, fund-raising and local control of independent
schools.   Has a useful bibliography.

125.   Ward, Leo R.   Federal Aid to Private Schools.   Westmin-
ister, Md.: Newman Press, 1964.   200p.
   Father Ward believes that federal aid to private schools is
a part of the right to freedom of expression by parents.   The book
is well documented and contains a bibliography.

126.   Ware, Martha L., and Remmlein, Madeline K.   School Law.
Fourth edition.   Danville, Ill.: Interstate Printers and Publishers,
Inc., 1979.   583p.
   A presentation of existing laws pertaining to schools designed
for teacher-training institutions rather than law schools.   References
relating to private education are to be found under such entries as
"admission and attendance", transportation at public expense and
"textbooks and curriculum".

127.   Wilkenson, Doreen H.   Community Schools: Education for
Change.   Boston: National Association of Independent Schools, 1973.
50p.
   A brief but informative survey of the community school, including thoughts on parental involvement, teaching methods in urban
areas and the philosophy of the community school.

128.   Winter, Nathan.   Jewish Education in a Pluralist Society:
Samson Benderly and Jewish Education in the United States.   New
York: New York University Press, 1966.   262p.
   A comprehensive review of the historical aspects of Jewish
education in the U.S., present status and the contributions made by
Samson Benderly in promoting Jewish schools.

129.   Yearbook of School Law. Edited by Philip K. Piele.   Topeka,
Kan.: National Organization of Legal Problems of Education, 1950-.
   A reference, now in its 30th year, containing state appelate

and federal court decisions affecting the operation and governance of public elementary and secondary schools. However, a discussion of similar legislation, related to private education is included each year. Chapters are individually written by persons experienced in school law.

130.   Zeidner, Nancy L.   Private Elementary and Secondary Education: A Bibliography of Selected Publications (1950-1974).   Washington, D.C.:   Council for American Private Education, 1976.   104p.
        A comprehensive list of books and pamphlets published or reprinted in the U.S. and England for the time period indicated.   Entries are divided into nine major sections and include such publications as teaching materials.   Annotations consist of alphabetical listings of the subjects covered in each item.   Author and subject index are combined in one.

II. FEDERAL AND STATE GOVERNMENT PUBLICATIONS

131. Bricknell, Henry M., and others. Nonpublic Education in Massachusetts: The Report of the Commonwealth of Massachusetts Special Commission to Study Public Financial Aid to Nonpublic Primary and Secondary Schools and Certain Related Matters. New York: Institute for Educational Development, 1971. 254p.
    A report on private education in Massachusetts in regard to decline in enrollments, financial condition of the schools, the quality and status of teachers. Alternative forms of public aid to private schools are also presented in this report.

132. _____. Nonpublic Education in Rhode Island: Alternatives for the Future. Providence: Rhode Island Special Commission to Study the Entire Field of Education, 1969. 226p.
    This study deals mainly with the Catholic school system in the state. Information is given on the historical precedents, school plants, teaching methods and public aid for these schools.

133. Center for the Study of Public Policy. Education Vouchers: A Report on Financing Elementary Education by Grants to Parents. Submitted to the Office of Economic Opportunity. Washington, D.C.: U.S. Office of Economic Opportunity, 1970. 348p.
    Research directed by Christopher Jencks and others. The advantages and disadvantages of vouchers as helping low-income families are discussed and a plan by which such a program could become a reality is presented.

134. Cohen, Wilbur, Jr., and others. The Financial Implications of Changing Patterns of Nonpublic School Operations in Chicago, Detroit, Milwaukee and Philadelphia. Submitted to the President's Commission on School Finance. Washington, D.C.: President's Commission on School Finance, 1971-. 239p.
    The "changing patterns" discussed in this report include environmental influences, demographic changes, racial attitudes, state aid to private schools and teacher supply.

135. Colorado. Governor's Study Committee on Nonpublic Schools. Final Report . . . Nonpublic Schools, Part II. Denver, 1971. 19p.
    A review of the developments in the state's private schools, the financial impact of nonpublic school closures and existing state aid to the private schools. Materials illustrated with charts and graphs.

136.   Cooper, Bruce S. Free and Freedom Schools: A National Survey of Alternative Programs. Submitted to the President's Commission on School Finance. Washington, D.C.: President's Commission on School Finance, 1971. 138p.

A consideration of all aspects of alternative education programs, the costs involved, legal implications, function of this type of schooling, the currivulum and future perspectives.

137.   Council for American Private Education.   Handbook for Private School Administrators for Effective Participation in Federal Education Programs Administered by the U.S. Office of Education. Washington, D.C.: U.S. Govt. Printing Office, 1974. 46p.

Guidance for the private school administrator whose school is involved in the numerous federal programs provided through the Elementary and Secondary Education Act of 1965 and other legislation.

138.   Erickson, Donald A. Crisis in Illinois Nonpublic Schools: Final Research Report of the Elementary and Secondary Nonpublic Schools Study Commission, State of Illinois, December 29, 1970. Springfield: State of Illinois Study Commission, 1970. 438p.

A detailed study with useful bibliographic footnotes of the role of the state in its nonpublic school system. Reviews some of the problems in dealing with enrollments and finances.

139.   . Recent Enrollment Trends in the U.S. Nonpublic Schools: Final Report to the National Institute of Education. Washington, D.C.: The Institute, 1977. 116p.

This survey examines recent (i.e., since 1965) and projected enrollment trends and explores the causes and consequences of these trends. One major conclusion: The rising demand for nonpublic schools is the result of public disenchantment with the present system, particularly in the deep South and Southwest.

140.   . The Three R's of Nonpublic Education in Louisiana: Race, Religion and Region. Submitted to the President's Commission on School Finance. Washington, D.C.: President's Commission on School Finance, 1972. 315p.

The implications for nonpublic education in Louisiana are considered in relation to the Elementary and Secondary Education Act of 1965. Also appraised are the role of religion in private education, race relations in various parts of the state and innovations in Catholic education.

141.   Fahey, Frank J. Economic Problems of Nonpublic Schools.
Submitted to the President's Commission on School Finance.   Notre
Dame, Ind.:   Office for Educational Research, 1971.   660p.
     A comprehensive review of the financial problems of nonpub-
lic schools, including those in the church-related diocesan system.
The cost of absorbing nonpublic school children into the public
schools is also discussed.

142.   The Financial Implications of Changing Patterns of Nonpublic
School Operations in Chicago, Detroit, Milwaukee and Philadelphia.
Submitted to the President's Commission on School Finance.   Ann
Arbor: University of Michigan, 1971.   239p.
     The "changing patterns" of nonpublic school operations con-
cern demographic make-up of the cities, changing neighborhoods,
and the ability to finance nonpublic schools in the inner city.

143.   Foerster, Janet S. Public Aid to Nonpublic Education.   Submitted to the President's Commission on School Finance.   Washington, D.C.:   U.S. Gov. Printing Office, 1971.   91p.
     The public aid studied in this report are: health services,
shared facilities, state aid, instructional materials, vouchers, tax
adjustments and shared-time with public schools.

144.   Ford, Elinor R. The Role and Significance of Nonpublic Education in New York State.   Albany: New York State Education Department, 1977.   52p.   (Occasional Paper No. 25)
     Information on enrollment trends and the amount of public
funds saved by the existence of the nonpublic schools.   The report
also points out how private schools provide the quality education and
diversity needed for educational opportunity.

145.   Freeman, Roger A.   "Income Tax Credits for Tuitions and
Gifts in Nonpublic School Education. " In Tax Credits for Education.
Submitted to the President's Commission on School Finance (Washington, D.C.:   President's Commission on School Finance, 1971), p.
23-58.
     The noted economist presents his views on tutition and tax
decuctions for parents of private school children and other deduc-
tions and exemptions available.

146.   Gary, Louis R.   The Collapse of Nonpublic Education:
Rumor or Reality?   The Report on Nonpublic Education in the State
of New York for the New York State Commission on the Quality,
Cost and Financing of Elementary and Secondary Education.   New
York: Implications Research, 1971.   2 vols.

Among the twelve contributors to this report are Donald A. Erickson, George LaNoue and Leo Pfeffer.   Main subjects treated: scope of private education in N.Y. State, declining revenues, dual enrollments, federal aid to private schools, Supreme Court decisions affecting private education.

147.   Issues of Aid to Nonpublic Schools.   4 vols.   Edited by Donald A. Erickson and George F. Madous.   Final report submitted to the President's Commission on School Finance.   Chestnut Hill, Mass.:   Center for Field Research and School Services, Boston College, June 1, 1971.
The four volumes are entitled: I.   Economic and Social Issues of Educational Pluralism; II.   Social and Religious Sources of the Crisis in Catholic Schools; III.   Public Assistance Programs for Nonpublic Schools; IV.   Appendices.   (A 35 page summary of these four volumes is available from the Center.)

148.   Maxwell, James A. , and Weinstein, Bernard L.   "A Tax Credit for Certain Educational Expenses. "   In Tax Credits for Education, submitted to the President's Commission on School Finance (Washington, D.C.:   The Commission, 1971), 23p.
A brief historical perspective of tax credits for educational expenses and the administrative problems that would arise in establishing such a program.

149.   New York (City).   Department of City Planning.   Three Out of Ten: The Nonpublic Schools of New York City.   New York, 1972. 287p.
A survey that could serve as a model for other city planners who wish to make a similar study.   Information covers all aspects of the nonpublic schools in operation, including ethnic composition of these schools, accreditation, state and federal aid.

150.   Nuccio, Vincent.   Notes and Working Papers Concerning the Administration of Programs Authorized Under Title I of the Elementary and Secondary Education Act of 1965:   Program Participation of Nonpublic School Children.   Phase I.   Final Report.   Prepared for the Subcommittee on Education of the Committee on Labor and Public Welfare, U.S. Senate.   Washington, D.C.:   U.S. Gov. Printing Office, December 1967.   159p.   (At head of title: 90th Congress, 1st session.   Committee Print.)

A collection of scholarly notes and working papers that provides an insight into all of the possibilities offered to private schools through the titles of the Elementary and Secondary Education Act of 1965.

151.   Title I ESEA: Participation of Private School Children.   A Handbook for State and Local School Officials.   Washington, D.C.: U.S. Gov. Printing Office, 1971.   52p.
This handbook describes all of the benefits to be gained by the private school student in the Elementary and Secondary Education Act of 1965 and the problems that will be encountered in implementing this program by state and local officials.

152.   U.S. Congress.   House.   Committee on Labor and Public Welfare.   Aid to Nonpublic Education, 1971-1972. Hearings.   92nd Congress, First and Second Sessions ... December 2, 1971 and January 11, 1972.   Washington, D.C.: U.S. Gov. Printing Office, 1972.   526p.
Testimony by leaders in education, religion and other segments of society included such topics as: justification for religious education (Catholic and Jewish), church-state relations, pluralism in American society, racial integration and shared time.

153.   U.S. Congress.   House.   Committee on Ways and Means. Hearings on Tax Credits for Nonpublic Education.   92nd Congress, 2nd Session, August and September 1972.   In three parts.   Washington, D.C.: U.S. Gov. Printing Office, 1972.
Testimony by such prominent persons as E. Doerr, William Brickman and Archbishop Terrence Cooke (now Cardinal).   Discussion related to constitutional questions on tax credits, probable impact of such legislation on parochial schools, alleged potential racial, academic and other imbalances in public schools should there be Federal support of private schools.

154.   U.S. Department of Health, Education, and Welfare.   Church-State Relations: The Legality of Using Public Funds for Private Schools.   By Michael R. Smith and Joseph E. Bryson.   Washington, D.C.: The Department, 1972.   89p.
A position paper from the Department outlining the government's stand on aid to church-related schools.

155.   _____.   Office of the Assistant Secretary for Planning and Evaluation.   Tuition Tax Credits for Elementary and Secondary Education: Some New Evidence on Who Would Benefit.   By Martha J. Jacobs.   Washington, D.C.: The Department, 1979.   18p.   (Technical Analysis Paper No. 7.)

This report contains data from the 1978 October supplement to the Current Population Survey that shows, for the first time, who attends private schools and what tuition fees they pay. From such estimates, it can be determined "who would benefit."

156.   . Office of the General Counsel. Memoranda Discussing the Constitutionality of S. 1021 and the Constitutionality of Loans to Private Schools, Including Sectarian Institutions. Washington, D.C.: U.S. Gov. Printing Office, 1961. 84p.
This memo defines the government's position on the Constitutionality of loans to private schools and also discusses training of guidance counselors, nonbook media, special education programs and student testing.

157. U.S. Library of Congress, Legislative Reference Service. A History of Proposals Which Have Received Consideration by the Congress of the United States (1789-1960). Report Prepared for the Committee on Education and Labor, House of Representatives, 87th Congress, Washington, D.C.: U.S. Gov. Printing Office, 1961. 72 p.
Proposals concerning federal aid and assistance to private education are included in this survey.

158.   . Proposed Federal Promotion of "Shared Time" Education: A Digest of Relevant Literature and Summary of Pro and Con Arguments. Washington, D.C.: U.S. Gov. Printing Office, 1963. 46p.
Useful as an assessment of opinions on "shared time" for that period and the persons expressing those opinions.

159. U.S. National Center for Educational Statistics. Nonpublic Elementary and Secondary Schools, 1965-1966. Washington, D.C.: U.S. Gov. Printing Office, 1968. 50p.
Provides statistics on enrollments, church-related and secular schools, student-teacher ratios. Useful for comparative purposes.

160.   . Nonpublic Schools in Large Cities: 1970-1971 Edition. By Diane B. Gertler. Washington, D.C.: The Center, 1974. 46p.
Data presented describes some of the characteristics and status of nonpublic schools in 43 large cities of the U.S. This survey includes schools for the handicapped, military schools and private college preparatory institutions.

161. _____. Private Schools in American Education. By Roy Nehrt. Washington, D.C.: U.S. Gov. Printing Office, 1981. 56p.
A presentation of abstracts of statistical information about private elementary and secondary schools gleaned from recent surveys made by the National Center. A brief history of the American private school is also given.

162. _____. Statistics of Public and Nonpublic Elementary Day Schools, 1968-1969. By Diane B. Gertler and Linda A. Barker. Washington, D.C.: U.S. Gov. Printing Office, 1971. 62p.
Useful for comparative purposes. Data similar to that gathered in earlier surveys by the U.S. Office of Education.

163. U.S. National Institute of Education. The Private High School Today. By Susan Abramowitz, E. Ann Stackhouse, and others. Washington, D.C.: U.S. Gov. Printing Office, 1980. 169p.
The results of a survey of 600 private schools, undertaken by the National Institute and the Council for American Private Education and designed to serve as a companion volume to an earlier study on public schools called High School '77. All aspects of the private high school were covered such as student body, programs offered, management and policies. A special chapter on the Catholic high school is given. Numerous charts illustrate statistical data.

164. U.S. Office of Education. Directory of Secondary Day Schools, 1951-52. Showing Accredited Status, Enrollment, Staff and Other Data. By Mabel C. Rice. Washington, D.C.: U.S. Gov. Printing Office, 1952. 169p.
Useful for historical and comparative purposes. Listing includes secular and church-related schools.

165. _____. Dual Enrollment in Public and Nonpublic Schools. Washington, D.C.: U.S. Gov. Printing Office, 1965. (Circular No. 772.)
A review of those schools implementing the shared-time principle. Statistics mostly cover enrollment figures.

166. _____. Nonpublic Secondary Schools: A Directory, 1960-61, Showing Accreditation Status, Enrollment, Classroom Teachers and Other Data. By Diane B. Gertler and Leah W. Ramsey. Washington, D.C.: U.S. Gov. Printing Office, 1963. 106p.
A comprehensive listing, useful for comparative purposes.

167. _____. Nonpublic Secondary Schools: A Directory, 1960-61, Showing Accreditation Status, Enrollment, Classroom Teachers and Other Data. By Diane B. Gertler and Leah W. Ramsey. Washington, D.C., U.S. Gov. Printing Office, 1963. 106p.
    A comprehensive listing, useful for comparative purposes.

168. _____. State Law Relating to Transportation and Textbooks for Parochial School Students. By August W. Steinhibler and Carl J. Sokolowski. Washington, D.C.: 1966. 80p. (Circular No. 795.)
    For an update on such state laws see Helen M. Jessison's State and Federal Laws Relating to Nonpublic Schools [item 118].

169. _____. Statistics of Nonpublic Elementary Schools, 1961-62. Washington, D.C.: U.S. Gov. Printing Office, 1962-. (Published as a Circular.)
    Statistics of this type, prior to 1960, were published as chapters in the Office's Biennial Survey of Education in the U.S. Information includes enrollments, types of schools, etc.

170. _____. Statistics of Nonpublic Secondary Schools; Type of School, Enrollment and Staff, 1960/61- . Washington, D.C.: U. S. Gov. Printing Office, 1960/61-.
    The statistics on nonpublic secondary education, as in the case of the nonpublic elementary schools, appeared in the Office's Biennial Survey of Education, prior to 1960.

171. _____. Subject Offerings and Enrollments, Grades 9-12, Nonpublic Secondary Schools, 1961-62. By Diane B. Gertler. Washington, D.C.: U.S. Gov. Printing Office, 1965. 167p. (Circular No. 745)
    Useful for comparative purposes, particularly in the subjects offered in the schools at the beginning of the 1960's.

172. U. S. President's Panel on Nonpublic Education. Nonpublic Education and the Public Good. Report submitted to the President's Commission on School Finance. Washington, D.C.: President's Commission on School Finance, April 14, 1972. 58p.
    The President's Panel on Nonpublic Education was created by President Richard Nixon as a part of his President's Commission on School Finance. This final report is divided into three main headings: "Popular Fallacies as to the Role of Nonpublic Schools," "The Nature of the Crisis in Nonpublic Schools" and "Perils of Public Policy."

III. ARTICLES IN PERIODICALS

173. Beer, Ethel. "Is the American School System Democratic?" Social Studies 41 (Dec. 1950) 345-8.
     An overall view of the dual system of education in America, public and private and describing the features that make each distinctive. Because the private school is costly, the author believes that wealth and privilege contribute to a greater separation of the two systems of schooling.

174. "Black Reflections on the Independent School." Independent School Bulletin 30 (Dec. 1970) 9-20.
     A group of four articles are given under the above title. They represent the opinions of students, a teacher and a trustee on their experiences as a minority group in an independent school.

175. Blum, Virgil C. "Quality Education for Inner-City Minorities." Vital Speeches 44 (April 1, 1978) 362-6.
     High unemployment among inner-city Blacks is due to illiteracy, stemming from low quality education. Blum thinks that this cycle can be reversed by giving educational vouchers to Blacks, whereby they are able to use them for a better education, be it in a public or private school.

176. Bolmeier, E.C. "Court Decisions and Enrollment Trends in Public and Nonpublic Schools." Elementary School Journal 51 (Oct. 1950) 70-6.
     Factors that influence enrollment trends in public and private schools. The author discusses those court decisions that have "gone a long way in promoting the growth of nonpublic education."

177. Bregman, Susan. "Sports in the Independent School." Independent School 37, 3 (1978) 1-17.
     The opinions of 30 private schools as to the best method of helping the individual develop his potential in athletics and as a person.

178. Brewster, Kingman. "Looking Ahead." Independent School Bulletin 33, 3 (1973) 34-6.
     The former president of Yale University considers three ele-

ments most important to successful private education: the quality
and diversity of its student body, the school's background and experience and the faculty members.

179.   Brickman, William W. "Public Aid to Religious Schools?"
Religious Education 55 (July-Aug. 1960) 279-88.
   This article is one in a symposium on "Religion and Public
Education." It expresses the views of Jewish groups and clergy on
the question of public funds for church-related schools.

180.   Brooks, John J.   "Independent School: A Public Resource."
Childhood Education 29 (March 1953) 307-8.
   The author believes that the independent school, when prop-
erly run, acts as a gadfly to the "great ponderous body of public education", spurring it on to greater activity. He cites many examples
to prove his opinions.

181.   Butler, Paul.   "Government Aid to the Private School."
Catholic Mind 59 (May-June 1961) 205-15.
   Reprint of an address given by the former Chairman of the
Democratic National Committee.   Butler reviews the need for finan-
cial assistance to Catholic schools, and the Supreme Court decisions
maintaining the status of church-related schools through the First
Amendment that made their establishment possible.

182.   Buttenheim, Peter V.   "Lifelong Learning." Independent
School 37, 4 (1978) 57-60.
   Declining secondary private school enrollments expected in
the mid-1980's will cause financial hardship for many institutions.
Buttenheim suggests that the 800 member schools of the National
Association of Independent Schools could alleviate some of this finan-
cial difficulty by using their facilities for adult education.

183.   Carr, Ray, and Hayward, Gerald C.   "Education by Chit:
An Examination of Voucher Proposals." Education and Urban Society
3 (Feb. 1970) 179-91.
   Two educators from the University of California at Berkeley
examine voucher proposals as offered by Milton Friedman, Christopher Jencks and Theodore Sizer, with Phillip Whitten, Henry Levin
and James S. Coleman.

184.   Carter Jimmy, President. (Letter) Momentum 9 (May 19-
78) 3.
   Excerpts from one of President Carter's 1976 campaign ad-
dresses in which he supports national programs for nonpublic schools
and the right of Americans to choose church-related education for
their children.

185.   Chlopinski, K., and Parsell, R. "Sociological Study of Behavior Deviations in the Private Schools of the U.S.A." Nervous Child 10, 3-4 (1954) 425-46.
       The results of a study to discover how schools handle such misconduct as cheating, theft, vandalism, forgery. Questionnaire returns from 364 private schools were analyzed and form the basic data of this report.

186.   Cohen, David K., and Ferrar, Eleanor. "Power to the Parents? The Story of Education Vouchers." The Public Interest No. 48 (Summer 1977) 72-77.
       An analysis of educational vouchers and how the idea took hold in government, particularly through the efforts of the now defunct U.S. Office of Economic Opportunity. The authors relate the failure of the voucher program in local communities and cite the Alum Rock (Calif.) experience as an example.

187.   "Coleman II: The Data Are In." CAPE Outlook No. 71 (May 1981) 1-2.
       An examination of the 271 page draft report by James R. Coleman entitled Public and Private Schools. The data from which the newest Coleman report was made evolved from a study of 1,016 high schools and 58,728 students. Coleman stresses the achievements of private school students compared to those of public schools.

188.   Consedine, William R. "Constitutionality of the Inclusion of Church-Related Schools in Federal Aid to Education." Georgetown Law Journal 50 (1961) 397-455.
       A study done by the legal department of the National Catholic Welfare Conference. Contents: Part I: "The Education Crisis and National Survival; Part II: "The Constitution and Church-Related Education."

189.   Cookson, Peter W., Jr. "Teacher Evaulation in Independent Schools: An Empirical Investigation." Independent School 39 (May 1980) 47-54.
       Methods used for teacher evaluation in private schools. The traditionally informal procedures are changing in favor of more effective formal ones.

190.   Coons, John E., and Sugarman, Stephen D. "Choice in Education: With Questions and Answers." Center Magazine 13 (Sept. 1978) 46-58.
       The authors along with Thomas V. Martin and Gerald Hedden give their views on the options that parents and children have if educational vouchers were to be granted for private schooling.

191.   . "Vouchers for Public Schools." Inequality in Education 15 (1973) 60.
        What could be accomplished by an educational voucher program.   Topics covered include "governance and independent schools" and "starting new schools and ending unpopular ones."

192.   Corkran, John R.   "Shake the Helping Hand: Tips on How Independent Schools Can Influence Local and State Government Policy. CASE Currents 6 (May 1980) 36-8.
        Suggestions for developing good relations with local and state governments that provide such "helping hands" as funding programs, tax exemptions and civil rights legislation.

193.   Cornell, Francis G.   "Federal Aid Is a Religious Issue." School Executive 72 (June 1953) 47-9.   Comment by R. H. Schenk, S.J., 72 (August 1953) 13.
        The rejection of the "Catholic view" that parochial and other church-related schools have a right to public financial aid. A reply to Cornell is to be found in a letter to the editor by the Jesuit educator R. H. Schenk.

194.   Costanzo, Joseph F., S. J.   "Ribicoff on Federal Aid to Education." Thought, Fordham University Quarterly 36 (Winter 19-61) 485-536.
        A critical study of a memorandum submitted to the Senate Subcommittee on Education, March 28, 1961 by the former Secretary of Health, Education and Welfare (Abraham Ribicoff). The memorandum discusses the constitutionality of loans to private schools and gives a summary of existing federal legislation benefitting sectarian institutions.

195.   Dandridge, William L. "Recruiting Minority Teachers for Independent Schools." Independent School 38 (Dec. 1978) 8-11.
        Specific strategies that might be used in recruiting minority faculty members for private schools.

196.   Deal, Terrance E.   "An Organizational Explanation of the Failure of Alternative Secondary Schools." Educational Researcher 4 (April 1975) 10-17.
        Explanations as to why the "experiments in secondary schooling" have, to a large extent, failed in their mission. Deal provides two case studies to illustrate his convictions.

197.   Davis, Gerald N.   "Educational Opportunities for Black Americans at Independent Schools." Crisis 85, 7 (1978) 231-6.
        The results of data collected on black independent school graduates, showing that 99 per cent entered college, with the majority accepted at prestigious institutions.

198. DiPerna, Paula. "Tuition Tax Credits: Relief for Which Class?" Nation 113 (August 1978) 143-6.

The tuition tax credit proposal sponsored by Senators Packwood and Moynihan would ignore the poor, while providing aid for the rich, according to DiPenna. She also presents other statements by those who support her views and oppose the Packwood-Moynihan proposal.

199. Dodson, Dan W. "Foreword: Democracy and Private Education." Journal of Educational Sociology 30 (April 1957) 337-8.

In order for a private school to justify its existence in a democracy it must, according to the author, fill all, or partially, four roles: 1) experimental--initiate programs that public schools cannot do; 2) yardstick--serve as a measure by which public education can be compared; 3) creative--provide programs with moral or spiritual values; 4) leadership--make a definite impact on the mainstream of education.

200. Doerr, Edd. "Federal Parochiaid Again." Humanist 39 (July 1979) 61.

The "new campaign" to lobby Congress to pass the Packwood-Moynihan bill for tuition tax credits and the Roth-Ribicoff bill for tuition-grant parochiaid (aid to parochial schools). Although ruled unconstitutional by the Supreme Court in 1973, organizers of the lobby believe that the passage of such legislation will give the Supreme Court a chance to "reverse itself".

201. _____. (Letter) Harper's 128 (June 1978) 4ff.

This lengthy letter is a rebuttal of the stand that Senator Moynihan takes on the tuition tax credit bill he has co-sponsored with Senator Packwood. Doerr believes that Moynihan has distorted and omitted certain facts that should be made known.

202. _____. "The Packwood-Moynihan Boondoggle." Humanist 38 (Jan. 1978) 51-2; Part II: (March 1978) 56

According to Doerr, the Packwood-Moynihan tax credit bill would be costly and unconstitutional, and would proliferate nonpublic schools while destroying the public school system.

203. _____. "The Voucher Menace." Humanist 38 (Nov. 1978) 51-2.

A critique of the book Education and Choice by John E. Coons and Stephen D. Sugarman, containing plans for parochiaid. Doerr contends that this plan ignores all Supreme Court rulings and would force tax payers to support religious instruction in schools.

204. Eckelberry, R. H. "Independent School in American Demo-

cracy." (Editorial) Journal of Higher Education 27 (May 1956) 280-1.
A brief résumé and comment on the conference held at Marquette University (May 8-10, 1956) on "The Role of the Independent
School in American Democracy." Although a success in every way,
Eckelberry believes that the conference was too dominated by discussions on Catholic education while neglecting other types of independent schooling.

205.   Editorial.   "Discrediting Tax Credits."   America 116 (April
29, 1978) 334-5.
A summary of the main arguments for and against tax credit
for education, with the "pro" group overriding the others.

206.   Evans, M. Stanton.   "The Tuition War."   National Review
23 (Jan. 20, 1978) 96.
Because of inflation, private school enrollments have de-
clined and the tuition tax credit would greatly remedy that.   Evans
also believes that the public could not afford greater enrollments in
the public school system and that private schools are needed to provide greater diversity in education.

207.   "Faculty Compensation and Tuition: The Perennial Question.
Independent School 38 (Feb. 1979) 31-2.
A question and answer format, dealing with the subjects of
teacher salaries and fringe benefits in relation to tuition.

208.   "Federal Aid and Catholic Schools."   Commonweal 79 (Jan.
31, 1964) 500-42.
A special issue devoted to all aspects of federal aid to
Catholic schools.   The articles are from 10 contributors, including
George N. Shuster, Martin Mayer and Neil G. McCluskey, S. J.

209.   Freeman, Roger A.   "Tax Credits and the School Aid Dead-
lock."   Catholic World 194 (Jan. 1962) 201-8.
The legal, political and educational implications of federal
aid to private schools.   Freeman proposes tax credits as the solu-
tion, rather than direct government loans or grants.

210.   Fuller, Edgar.   "Government Financing of Public and Private Schools."   Phi Delta Kappan 47 (March 1966) 365-72.
The disturbing trends that concern our vast public expenditures for public and nonpublic education.   Fuller gives an assessment of the possible damages to public education if private institutions should gain additional federal funds.

211.   Gallagher, William P., and Baisinger, Grace.   "Tax Credits for Private Schools: Pro and Con Discussion: Interview."   U. S.

News and World Report 45 (May 1, 1978) 69-70.
        Opinions of a representative of Catholic School Parents and
the Coalition to Save Public Education on the subject of tax credits
for private school parents.

212.   Gauerke, Warren.   "Private School Plans and Racial Integration. "   School and Society 81 (April 30, 1955) 129-53.
        Plans for the creation for private schools to avoid integra-
tion, when presented to state legislators, provide them with an opportunity for a "oblique attack on the traditional separation of church
and state. " Gauerke maintains that these so-called private schools
are still supported by public funds and subject to the Supreme Court
decision on school integration.

213.   Gerstman, Leslie.   "Racial Integration in Non-Public
Schools. "   NOLPE School Law Journal 8, 2, (1979) 210-20.
        A presentation of the legal issues related to racial discrim-
ination in private schools such as, admission policies and the legality of proposed revenue procedures for tax-exempt schools.

214.   Gilbert, Steven W. "Television, Families and Schools. "   Independent School 37, 3, (1978) 29-35.
        An evaluation of television programs and their impact on
parents and students.   The author suggests ways for independent
teachers and administrators to provide guidance on this issue.

215.   Handlin, Oscar, and Miller, William I.   "Two Views on Aid
to Catholic Schools. "   Catholic World 193 (July 1961) 216-24.
        Two essays written in reply to certain passages from the
book We Hold These Truths by John C. Murray, S. J.   The arguments center mainly upon the constitutionality of government aid to
Catholic schools.

216.   Hardiman, Edward J.   "Federal Aid to Education--For Some
or For All?"   Temple Law Quarterly 23 (Jan. 1950) 227-31.
        A legal analysis of three Senate proposals: the Thomas,
Barden and Fogarty bills, introduced at the 1st Session of the 81st
Congress (1949).   The author describes the "furor" created by these
proposals, as they either ignored public funds for nonpublic schools
(Barden), gave blanket coverage for them (Fogarty) or offered a solu-
tion somewhere in between (Thomas).

217.   Heely, Allan V.   "Case for Private Schools. "   School Executive 75 (Oct. 1955) 19-21.
        A former headmaster of the Lawrenceville School states the
aims and objectives of the ideal private school, including the need to
train students in the service of society.

218. Heeney, Brian. "Tom Brown's New World: North American Versions of the English Public School." Journal of Educational Thought 12 (Dec. 1978) 219-27.
          Comparison of American and Canadian independent schools through the reviews of two books: The Elite Schools by Leonard Baird and A Question of Privilege by Carolyn Gossage. The scho described in these works are used as the basis for comparison.

219. Heller, Harry. "Independent School as a Center for Teac. Education." Journal of Educational Sociology 30 (April 1957) 381-4.
          To be an effective center for teacher training, an independent school must have a definite philosophy of education, the freed⌐ to teach and ability to transmit quality in education.

220. Hollings, Ernest F. "The Case Against Tuition Tax Cred its." Phi Delta Kappan 60 (Dec. 1978) 277-79.
          Senator Hollings points out what he believes to be the falla cies of the Packwood-Moynihan bill for tuition tax credits. He also states that it is the duty of government to provide for public housing only and to leave private education alone.

221. Holt, Don, and others. "School Tax Credits?" Newsweel 44 (Dec. 26, 1977) 76.
          The pros and cons of tax credits for education. Don Holt states that such credits would appeal to parents already pinched by rising school costs, while those opposed believe that two-thirds of the tax credit benefits would go to wealthy families.

222. Howe, Harold, Jr. "Turning the Past to the Future: The Job of Trusteeship". Independent School 38 (Oct. 1978) 7-9.
          A former U.S. Commissioner of Education reviews the pro lems of maintaining equity and excellence in the private school.

223. Jencks, Christopher. "Is the Public School Obsolete?" The Public Interest 2 (Winter 1966) 18-27.
          One of the greatest problems in American education is that of maintaining a school system in the inner-city. Jencks gives the advantages of providing private education for slum children and way in which private initiative for this system can be developed.

224. _____. "Private Schools for Black Children." Education Digest 34 (March 1969) 1-4.
          The digest of an article that first appeared in the Nov. 3, 1968 issue of the New York Times Magazine. Jencks presents an "alternative" to the inadequate schooling that black children in large public school systems now receive, by which the black community

would organize its own private school system and seek federal and state support.

225. Kauper, Paul G. "Church and State: Cooperative Separa-sm." Michigan Law Review 60 (1961) 1-40.
     The author, a professor of law at the University of Michigan, eviews all of the past debates held on questions of church-state re-tions in the U.S., including the use of public funds for church-re-ted schools. Supreme Court cases are cited.

226. Kearney, Vincent S. "Of Many Things." America 116 (Oct. 3, 1978) 272.
     The defeat of the 1978 tax credit bill is due to anti-Catholic gotry as well as to the public school lobby that fears quality com-etition from private schools. Kearney also believes that such legis-ation as a tax credit bill could be passed if enough Catholics fight r it.

227. Kemerer, Frank R. "A Call for Better Personnel Relations." idependent School 38 (Feb. 1979) 34-8.
     Effective school personnel practices for the independent chool, including policy statements setting forth terms and conditions or faculty, nonteaching staff, administrators and heads.

228. Kilborne, William S., Jr. "Education a la Carte." Indepen-ent School 39 (Dec. 1979) 15-7.
     Kilborne writes that the private day school should not try to mulate the boarding school in offering academic, athletic and art ac-ivities in addition to the regular curriculum. These should be sep-rated into "optional tracks", each with a separate tuition fee.

229. Kilpatrick, James J. "Tuition Grants and Trojan Horses." Nation's Business 68 (Oct. 1978) 17-8.
     The noted conservative journalist sees little difference be-ween tax credits and the indirect aid already received, because con-ributors to sectarian schools can deduct the amounts from taxable ncome. He also warns of the consequences for religious schools re-ceiving federal aid such as unwelcome federal regulations.

230. Knowles, Harvard, and Weber, David. "The School Com-munity as a Moral Environment." Independent School 38 (Dec. 1978) 13-7.
     Secular private schools may unwittingly stress the wrong values in their students, such as elitism, selfishness and smugness. Educators should also try to live by the moral values they profess.

231. Krughoff, Robert W. "Private Schools for the Public."

Education and Urban Society 2 (Nov. 1969) 54-79.
          An examination of the educational voucher proposal, its strengths, weaknesses and the impact it would have on large city public school systems.

232.   Lamborn, Robert L.   "Private Schools: In Support of Diversity."   National Elementary Principal 56, 6 (1977) 12-5.
          Private schools are joining forces in order to make themselves better understood, strengthen programs and to protect their diversity.

233.   Lancaster, John S.   "Fund Raising in the West."   Independent School Bulletin 34.   4 (1975) 49-53.
          Difficulties experienced on fund raising drives for private education.   Lancaster compares his experiences in the western U.S. with that of the Eastern seaboard.

234.   Lane, Bess.   "Should the Private School Apologize?"   Progressive Education 28 (Feb. 1951) 119-22.
          A parent and a teacher reminds us that private schools do exist in a nation where education is a public enterprise, and considers the question of why private schools should flourish.

235.   LaNoue, George R.   "The Politics of Education."   Teachers College Record 73 (Dec. 1971) 304-19.
          The concept of public and private education in America and the use of educational vouchers as a means of providing more efficient education with the least amount of public control.

236.   _____ .   "Religious Schools and 'Secular' Subjects."   Harvard Educational Review 32 (Summer 1962) 255-91.
          This article is based on a study of parochial school textbooks and challenges the constitutionality of providing public funds for the "secular subjects" (i.e. science, math, foreign languages) that are not always taught as such by parochial schools.

237.   Leary, Mary E.   "Another Chance for Vouchers?"   Commonweal 54 (Sept. 29, 1978) 613-23.
          The origins of the voucher concept for education.   Leary quotes Coons and Sugarman (see Item 190) on the purpose of vouchers: to put the power of choice of education in the hands of parents and discusses what may come of such power.

238.   Levin, Henry M.   "The Failure of the Public Schools and the Free Market Remedy."   The Urban Review 2 (June 1968) 32-7.
          A well documented article on alternative schooling and what could happen if the existing system of publicly operated schools were

to be replaced by a "market of private ones", supported by government vouchers.

239. Lewis, Lionel, and Wanner, Richard A. "Private Schooling and the Status Attainment Process." Sociology of Education 52 (April 1979) 99-112.
Findings of a study on the effects of a private school education on educational, occupational and earning attainments as compared to attendance at a public school. An analysis is given of the "private-school advantages" and its function in transmitting background relating to status attainment.

240. Liebarkin, Barbara. "Racial Attitudes of Whites in Public and Private Schools." Integrated Education 15, 6, (1977) 126-30.
White pupils in public and private schools of the Shepard Park Community (Washington, D.C.) were tested to verify the assumption that white children who have experienced racially mixed education become less prejudiced than their elders. The assumption was confirmed by this research.

241. Link, William R. "The Independent Day School in the Next Twenty-five Years: A Proposal for Survival." Independent School Bulletin 28 (Oct. 1968) 35-6.
In order for the day school to survive the "intensive and economic levelling" of American society in the future, it must give up values no longer relevant and create a society "less comfortable but more just."

242. Littleford, John C. "Cooperative Fund Raising--Will It Work?" Independent School 37, 4, (1978) 51-4.
The origin and development of the Minnesota Independent School Fund, Inc. (created in January, 1976) whose purpose is to promote corporate support of private secondary schools.

243. Lloyd, Francis V., Jr. "The Secondary School Principal; Or, Headmaster: How He Got There and How He Finds It." School Review 76 (March 1968) 92.
The major areas of concern for a successful school head and the results of a questionnaire sent to the 121 members of the Headmasters Association on the leadership role demanded of this position.

244. Lloyd, Gil B. "The Impact of the Brown Decision on Religion During the Past Twenty-Five Years." Negro Educational Review 30 (April-July 1979) 136-86.
The failures of the churches to integrate church-related schools and the causes of these failures.

245.   Look, Arnold E.   "The Public Relations of Independent Schools." Independent School Bulletin 1 (Nov. 1950) 15-7.
    Certain private school practices, such as fraudulent advertising and misuse of scholarship funds are cited as examples of the causes of poor relationships between public and private schools.

246.   Lubow, Arthur.   "Another Try for Vouchers? Theories of J. E. Coons and S. D. Sugarman." Newsweek 45 (Aug. 14, 1978) 64.
    Failure of the educational voucher plan, particularly at Alum Rock (Calif.) and a review of the theories of Coons and Sugarman on vouchers as expressed in their book Education and Choice.

247.   McCluskey, Neil G., S. J., and Butts, R. Freeman.   "Public Funds for Parochial Schools?" Teachers College Record 62 (Oct. 1960) 49-62.
    Two distinguished educators debate the thorny issue of using public funds for parochial school education.   Court decisions are used as authoritative sources for their arguments.

248.   McLean, Linda R.   "The Black Student in the White Independent School." Independent School Bulletin 28 (Feb. 1969) 68-73.
    Major problems confronting administrators and black students as found in the member schools of the National Association of Independent Schools.   These are centered on the effects of large and small numbers of blacks on campus, integrated rooming for girls and the needs of black students themselves.

249.   McMillan, William J.   "State Regulation of Private Schools." Headmaster, U.S.A. 4 (Dec. 1979) 13-5.
    Regulations for state control over private schools are expected to center primarily on literacy testing of students and minimum competency testing of teachers.

250.   Marver, James D.   "The Cost of Special Education in Nonpublic Schools." Journal of Learning Disabilities 9 (Dec. 1976) 651-60.
    Analysis of a survey of 61 nonpublic special education schools to determine their "market behavior."   The study demonstrated that such schools earn small profits, do not take unfair advantage of state subsidization and are not primarily motivated by monetary considerations.

251.   Meyers, John F.   "Beware of Supermarm." Momentum 10 (Oct. 1979) 4-6.
    Advice to Catholic educators to fight federal regulations(i.e. "Supermarm") of their schools.   These educators are also urged to

grant freedom and opportunity of education to the children of the
poor as well as to the more affluent.

252. Mooers, Jack D.   "Independent School Attendance and Social
Class Status."   Educational Studies 8, 3, (1977) 253-8.
      A review of some of the literature on independent schools
in the United States and Great Britain, that reveals the four major
functions of the private school in regard to academic standards,
peer group associations, "status validation" and opportunity for going
on to higher education.

253. Moquin, E. Michele.   "Constitutional Law--Establishment
Clause: No Tuition Grants, No Tax Benefits for Parents of Nonpublic School Children--Committee for Public Education and Religious
Liberty v. Nyquist, 413 U.S. 756 (1973)."   Washington Law Review
50, 3 (1975) 653-74.
      A legal analysis of the Supreme Court's treatment of New
York State's tuition reimbursement and tax exemption provisions
that were expected to equalize educational choice.   Moquin believes
that the decision is an unwarranted application of the constitutional
prohibition against the establishment of religion and offers alternatives available to state legislators.

254. "More Blacks, Less Integration.   Independent School Bulletin 29 (Oct. 1969) 14-8.
      Two articles are given under the above title: "Black Youth,
Black Nationalism and White Independent Schools" by William R.
Link and "Isn't This What Education Is All About?" by Robert M.
Sandoe.   Link makes suggestions on making education more produc-
tive for blacks and Sandoe's article contains correspondence
between himself and a 1946 alumnus concerning student racial problems.

255. Moynihan, Daniel P.   "The Case for Tuition Tax Credits."
Phi Delta Kappan 59 (Dec. 1978) 274-6.
      Senator Moynihan believes that the future of the public
school is secure and that tuition tax credits is just not a boon for
Catholic parents only.   He also wants Americans to be free of the
American public school monopoly and "his day in court" to prove
the constitutionality of the tax credit bill.

256. _____.   "Government and the Ruin of Private Education."
Harper's 128 (April 1978) 28-36.
      Moynihan clarifies the First Amendment and certain Sup-
reme Court rulings for the justification of the existence of private
schools and stresses the fact that tax credits for private education

will ensure the pluralism essential to our society and system of education.

257.   . "Why Private Schools Merit Public Aid: The Constitutional Case for Tuition Tax Credits." Independent School 37, 4 (1978) 18-21.
        The history and development of the dual system of education in America and the financial support of each. Moynihan discusses his reasons why he believes that parents of private school children should receive tuition tax credits.

258.   Nash, Nicholas. "The Public Face of Education's Private Sector." National Elementary Principal 56, 6 (1977) 22-6.
        Short-and-long-term social and economic pressures that appear to confront nonpublic schools, such as financial management, declining enrollments and public opinion of private schools.

259.   Nault, Richard L. and others. "Hard Times for Nonpublic Schools." National Elementary Principal 56, 6, (1977) 16-21.
        In spite of the economic and financial difficulties of the private school, there is a stable and growing number of parents who feel that the nonpublic school can provide the most suitable learning environment, especially in the parochial schools.

260.   Ogletree, Earl J. "The Waldorf Schools: An International School System." Headmaster U.S.A. 4 (Dec. 1979) 8-10.
        The curriculum design, aims and objectives of the Waldorf schools, a movement that includes 160 institutions internationally, of which 14 are in the United States.

261.   Orme, Charles H., Jr. "What Should We Expect of Secondary Education?" Independent School Bulletin 29 (May 1970) 5-6.
        Private schools must change from their original college preparatory role to one more meaningful in a technological society.

262.   Peterson, James W. "What's It Like in a Private School?" Phi Delta Kappan 61 (Sept. 1979) 22-3.
        A comparison of teaching experiences in public and private schools. Peterson emphasizes the shared values and goals of parents and teachers in nonpublic schooling.

263.   Pfeffer, Leo. (Letter) Harper's 23 (June 1973) 4ff.
        The author disagrees with Senator Daniel Moynihan's supposition that the Packwood-Moynihan bill for tuition tax credits is con-

stitutional.   He cites the Everson (1974) and Nyquist (1973) cases to
support his argument.

264.   "Pluralism in Education: Religious and Secular Patterns."
School Review 72 (Spring 1974) entire issue.
        A group of eight articles by various contributors.   Besides
discussing religious and secular patterns in nonpublic education, the
authors also consider the problems and importance of private schooling and the effects of Catholic school education in our democratic
society.

265.   Powell, Arthur G.   "Three Emerging Educational Issues."
Independent School 38 (Feb. 1979) 17-24.
        The three "issues" presented are increasing government in-
tervention in education, the changing American family and cycles of
education reform.   Powell describes the impact of these issues on
the conduct of private education in the United States.

266.   Pratt, Constance B.   "Educating the Whole Student."   Independent School 38 (May 1979) 15-9.
        Academic excellence and a concern for the individual stu-
dent are the two most frequently stated goals of independent schools.
Pratt discusses ways to achieve both of these often conflicting goals.

267.   "Private Education: A Tax Break?   Packwood-Moynihan
Bill."   Christianity Today 22 (April 21, 1978) 43.
        A listing of the supporters and non-supporters of the tui-
tion tax bill.   Those for the bill include mostly religious groups in
the Catholic, Protestant and Jewish communities.   Those opposing
the bill are representatives of labor, civil rights and education organizations.

268.   Richards, Carol R.   "Non-Public Schools Experience Mini-
Boom."   School Business Affairs 44, 1 (1978) 17-8.
        Discussion of the statistics on nonpublic school enrollments
as provided by the National Center for Educational Statistics.   Reasons are given for the upward swing of such enrollments.

269.   "Role of the Independent School in a Democratic Society."
Edited by V. Wagner.   Journal of Educational Sociology 30 (April
1957) 337-84.
        A special issue comprised of 15 articles on all aspects of
the independent school.   Subjects treated include the importance of
diversity in enrollments, contributions to public education and the
role of parents.

270.   Ryan, Carl J.   "Private Schools and Democracy."   Social

Studies 42 (May 1951) 210-2.
        A response to the article by Ethel Beer (See Item No. 173).
Ryan states that private schools exist because they represent the
freedom of choice that parents have to educate their children as they
see fit.

271.   "School Tax Credits: Making New Converts. " Christianity
Today 22 (Sept. 22, 1978) 37-8.
        Further names and views of supporters and opponents of the
tuition tax credit bill, including Jerry Falwell and Billy Graham as
for the bill and representative groups as the NEA, the NAACP and
various Jewish organizations in the opposition.

272.   Schuler, John G.   "Private Schools and Public Participation. "
Independent School Bulletin 29 (Dec. 1969) 7-9.
        Private school administrators and faculty should re-examine
their role in the light of the social changes now taking place in our
society.

273.   Seiden, Anne M.   "A New Breed of Parents. " Independent
School 37, 1 (1977) 15-6.
        Parental expectations in the education and training of their
children and how these can be realized through greater cooperation
between school and parents.

274.   Sheerin, John B.   "Conant and the Catholic Schools. " Catholic World 175 (June 1952) 161-5.
        In April 1952, James B. Conant, then President of Harvard
University, delivered an address in which he attacked the independent
school system of America, both private and parochial schools, at-
tributing to them characteristics unfavorable to our democratic society.   Sheerin refutes Conant's statements, concluding that democracy
cannot be divorced from religion and still survive.

275.   Sherry, Mary.   "Is State Aid the Saving Grace of Catholic
Education?" America 115 (April 9, 1977) 327-8.
        The means of survival for parochial schools is to look for
more constitutional means for obtaining state financial aid.

276.   Sizer, Theodore.   "The School and the State. " Independent
School 38 (Dec. 1978) 5-7.
        A review of federal government relationships to nonpublic
education and the hazards of over regulation in accepting government
grants.

277.   _____.   "Why the Public School?" National Elementary
Principal 56, 6 (1977) 6-11.

The purpose of the private school's existence is to join with publicly controlled education to form a system of depth, variety and choice. The independent school, furthermore, is not meant to serve as a sanctuary, means of escape or a ghetto for the rich.

278. Stair, Billy. "Renewed Struggle Between Public and Private Education: Tuition Tax Credits." Education Digest 43 (Dec. 1978) 7-10.
Problems likely to surface when tuition tax credits become a reality. Although it is unfair for parents of private school children to pay twice for their education, tax credits would promote pluralism and public schools would suffer enrollment loss.

279. Stern, David, and others. "Evolution at Alum Rock." The Review of Education 1 (1975) 309-19.
A critique of the Rand Corporation Report, A Public School Voucher Demonstration: The First Year at Alum Rock (Calif.). This research, sponsored by the National Institute of Education is evaluated by the author in all of its coverage of a system that eventually failed in theory and in practice.

280. Strasser, William C., Jr. "Education Act of 1965: Implications for Nonpublic Schools." Phi Delta Kappan 47 (Sept. 1965) 24-6.
Factors to be considered in the reassessment of the role of the nonpublic schools, in view of the federal regulations imposed upon them through the Elementary and Secondary Education Act of 1965.

281. Swomley, John M., Jr. "Tuition Tax Credits: Blank Check for Churches: Packwood-Moynihan Bill." Christian Century 95 (May 3, 1978) 462-4.
Swomley's main argument is that the bill would be too costly and that it would be unfair for non-Catholics to have to support Catholic schools.

282. Sylvester, Ben, Jr., and others. "Does Journalism Belong in Independent School Curriculum?" School Press Review 54 (Feb. 1979) 5-7, 10.
Comments from a panel comprised of independent school publications advisors on journalism programs, practices and teaching methods at their respective schools.

283. Taft, Robert Jr. "Independent Schools and Public Policy." CASE Currents 5 (July 1979) 6-8.
Contributions of independent schools to the American educational system and how these institutions fit into U.S. public policy on education. Financial support, equality of educational opportunity and quality of teaching are considered the "challenges" to our educational system.

284. _____ . "Private Schools and Public Policy." AGB Reports (Association of Governing Boards of Universities and Colleges Reports) 21 (Sept.-Oct. 1979) 42-4.
     The role of the independent school in solving some educational problems and for providing new ideas, diversity and special programs. Taft believes that tax credits for education would benefit both private and public education.

285. "Tax Credits and the Poor: Packwood-Moynihan Bill." America 69 (Feb. 18, 1978) 111.
     Views of supporters and opponents of the tax credit bill. Victor Solomon of the Congress of Racial Equality states that tax credits would enable poor black children to attend private schools and receive the education that public schools have failed in giving to them. Opponents such as President Carter and Joseph Califano offer dissenting views.

286. Teaford, Jon. "The Transformation of Massachusetts Education, 1670-1780." History of Education Quarterly 10, 3 (1970) 287-307.
     The grammar schools of the Massachusetts Colony laid the foundations for American private education. The author discusses how changing priorities forced the change from the traditional classical curriculum to support for vocational and English learning.

287. Van Geel, Tyll. "Parental Preferences and the Politics of Appending Public Education Funds." Teachers College Record 79 (Feb. 1978) 339-63.
     A rationale behind the educational voucher concept and previous federal government attempts to establish experimental voucher projects.

288. Vitullo-Martin, Thomas. "Providing Choice for Education." America 116 (Sept. 9, 1978) 128-30.
     Tax credits for private school parents as an incentive to remain in urban areas. If private schools were aided they could exert pressure on the public school system to reach for higher standards.

289. Walsh, J. H. "Wall of Separation: Only Public Schools Should Be Supported at Public Expense." National Education Association Journal 39 (Feb. 1950) 99-101.
     Why nonpublic schools should remain nonpublic with emphasis on America's historic commitment to separation of church and state.

290. Watt, A. J. "Freedom of Choice: For Whom? A Point

of View." Journal of Educational Administration 14 (Nov. 2, 1976)
261-9.
        Parents who select a school to reinforce their own beliefs
and attitudes often come in conflict with their children who have
their own ideas in selecting a school. The author discusses "freedom of choice" in such a situation.

291. Weber, William. "The Eclipse of Education Vouchers in
America: The East Hartford Case." Journal of Education 102 (May
1977) 36-42.
        The major components of the educational voucher program
initiated in East Hartford, Conn. and the factors that caused the
failure of the project such as the inability of the public to understand
the plan.

292. Wessler, Martin F. "The Distinctive Character of Church-
Related Schools." Headmaster U.S.A. 4 (Dec. 1979) 5-7.
        The seven distinct characteristics that should be present in
successful church-related schools, with the church itself as a major
component.

293. West, Ralph O. "Public Policy and the New England Academy." NASSP Bulletin 63 (Oct. 1979) 8-88. Same: Education Digest 45 (Jan. 1980) 39-42.
        Data from a study of 18 New England academies, with in-
sights on the role of the academy in today's society.

294. Wilcox, C.R. "Private Schools Look to the Future."
Southern Association Quarterly 11 (March 19, 1954) 39-46.
        Judging from conditions existing at the time, Wilcox makes
an assessment as to the character and success of the private school
in the future.

295. Wilkinson, Hugh C. "A Small Human School." Education
Canada 17 (Nov. 2, 1977) 14-21.
        The three indispensible attributes of a successful private
school: small size, extracurricular activities and a concern for the
ethical values of the students attending.

296. Will, George. "How to Make Our Schools Better: Tuition
Tax Credit Act." Newsweek 44 (Oct. 3, 1977) 104.
        The well known columnist states that the tuition tax credit
should be viewed in the same way as tax deductible contributions to
churches are viewed. He also compares the tax credit bill to an
anti-trust bill, since the government has a near monopoly on education and could promote the diversity that our Constitution permits.

IV.   UNPUBLISHED DOCTORAL DISSERTATIONS

297.   Adams, Joan F.   The Parochial-School Movement Within the Protestant Episcopal Church in the United States of America.   The American University, 1967

298.   Albert, Leo C.   A Comparative Study of Academic Achievement by Public, Private and Parochial School Graduates Attending Louisiana State University.   Louisiana State University, 1973

299.   Armstrong, Christopher F.   Privilege and Productivity: The Cases of Two Private Schools and Their Graduates.   University of Pennsylvania, 1974

300.   Barry, Laurence F.   A Study of Alternative Educational Futures for Parochial Schools Based on the Impact of Present Extra School Influences.   State University of New York at Albany, 1975

301.   Bauduccio, Anthony J.   The Potential Impact of the Parochial School on the Problems of Dual Enrollment.   University of Wyoming, 1971

302.   Becker, E. George.   The Impact of Social Change on the Lutheran Elementary Parochial School in Texas.   Texas A & M University, 1968

303.   Bothwell, H. Roger.   Moral Development of Seventh-Day Adventist High School Seniors Versus Other Parochial and Public High School Seniors.   Drake University, 1979

304.   Bowie, Dennis H.   A Study of Certain Factors Affecting Non-Enrollment in Selected Church-of-Christ Related Private Schools.   Memphis State University, 1968

305.   Brunner, James C.   Organization Variables and Teacher Self-Actualization in Public and Private Schools.   University of Texas at Austin, 1971

306.   Burton, Thomas.   Organization for the Control and Administration of the Independent School.   Harvard University, 1950

307.   Caire, Warren F.   A Study of Attitudes and Perceptions of Catholic School Parents and Teachers in New Orleans Parochial Schools as Compared to Catholic Schools in Washington, D.C. George Peabody College for Teachers of Vanderbilt University, 1979

308.   Caldwell, Cleon C.   The Development of Concepts Regarding the Use of Tax Funds for Public and Parochial Schools.   University of Minnesota, 1956

309.   Ciramella, Janet R.   An Analysis of the Tuition Tax Credit Movement and Implications for Public, Nonpublic and Private Basic Education.   University of Pittsburgh, 1980

310.   Cleveland, Allen D.   Alabama's Private, Nonsectarian Elementary and Secondary Schools in 1970.   Auburn University, 1970

311.   Clotfelder, Charles T.   An Economic Analysis of the Effect of School Desegregation on Residential Location and Private School Enrollment.   Harvard University, 1974

312.   Cole, John D.   Religion in Nonpublic Schools: A Selective Study, Comparing Pillar of Fire Schools With Those of Six Major Denominations.   University of Colorado at Boulder, 1978

313.   Cronin, David F.   A Study of Nonpublic Elementary and Secondary School Enrollment Within Massachusetts.   University of Massachusetts, 1974

314.   Cummings, Alban J.   Personal-Social Adjustment of Educational Achievement of West Indian Children in Selected Parochial Schools in New York City.   Fordham University, 1979

315.   Daele, Mary C.   The Participation of Nonpublic Schools and Nonpublic School Teachers in the Programs of the National Defense Education Act of 1958.   The Catholic University of America, 1963

316.   Damm, John S.   The Growth and Decline of Lutheran Parochial Schools in the United States, 1638-1962.   Columbia University, 1970

317.   DeBlaey, Gordon L.   A Comparison of Teacher Role Between Parochial and Public Schools.   Western Reserve University, 1970

318.   DePillo, George B.   Shared Time Relations of Public and Parochial Schools.   The University of Michigan, 1966

319. Dimauro, Arthur C. Private Special Education Services and the Public Interest. A Study of the Impact of Right to Education on Private Special Education Programs. Boston University, 1980

320. Duea, Jerry M. An Assessment of Provisions for Practical Teacher Education Experiences and Research in Public, Private and Laboratory Schools. Iowa State University, 1976

321. Dugan, Patrick B. State Aid to Nonpublic Schools in Missouri, 1959-1971. St. Louis University, 1972

322. Duhu, Robert. Differences Between Parochial and Public High School Teachers in Role Expectations and in Role Preferences. University of California, Los Angeles, 1971

323. Dykstra, Sidney. A Study of the Relationships of Nonpublic School Enrollment to the Approval of School Millage and Bond Proposals. The University of Michigan, 1964

324. Erekson, Owen H. The Impact of Private Education on the Provision of Public Education. University of North Carolina at Chapel Hill, 1980

325. Evans, F. David. A Study of the Desirability, Use and Helpfulness of Certain Selected Orientation Practices in Selected Private Schools. University of Kentucky, 1966

326. Evans, F. Laird. A Private School as Perceived by Socially and Emotionally Disturbed Students, Their Parents and Their Teachers. Lehigh University, 1976

327. Evearitt, Timonthy C. An Analysis of Why Parents Enroll Their Children in Private Christian Schools. Illinois State University, 1979

328. Farquhar, Robin H. Public School Administrators' Perceptions of Nonpublic School Effects on Public Schools. University of Chicago, 1967

329. Fay, Leo F. Catholics, Parochial Schools and Social Class: A Case Study, New School for Social Research, 1973

330. Fowle, David T. Study of Nonpublic Education in North Carolina at the Elementary and Secondary Level (Grades 1-12), 19-66-1971. Duke University, 1972

331. Franklin, Lewis G. Desegregation and the Rise of Private

Education. University of North Carolina at Greensboro, 1975

332. Funucan, J. Thomas. A Study of the Attitudes and Values of Catholic Parochial School Teachers. Loyola University of Chicago 1971

333. Gabert, Glen E. A History of the Roman Catholic Parochial School System in the United States: A Documentary Interpretation. Loyola University of Chicago, 1971

334. Ganss, Karl P. American Catholic Education in the 1960's: A Study of the Parochial School Debate. Loyola University of Chicago, 1979

335. Gerstman, Leslie S. Withdrawal of Blacks and Whites from Public to Nonpublic Elementary Schools in Minneapolis. University of Minnesota, 1979

336. Golding, Joanne. Analysis of the Legal Provisions of State Financial Aid to Nonpublic Schools for the Fifty States. Indiana State University, 1971

337. Gratiot, Margaret H. Why Parents Choose Nonpublic Schools: Comparative Attitudes and Characteristics of Public and Private School Consumers. Stanford University, 1979

338. Greenberg, Clementine K. The Educationally Handicapped Program: An Analysis and Comparison of Public and Private School Components. Claremont Graduate School, 1977

339. Greenfield, Gary J. A Study of Differences in Creative Thinking Between Public and Parochial School Children. Marquette University, 1972

340. Gryckiewicz, Jules F. State Aid to Nonpublic Schools and the First Amendment: A Historical and Philosophical Analysis of Supreme Court Decisions Affecting the Distribution of Government Benefits. University of Connecticut, 1980

341. Halpern, Stefanie J. Achievement and Home Environment of Negro Children from Urban Depressed Areas: An Investigation of the Relationship Between Higher and Lower Achievement in Parochial School and Selected Aspects of Home, Community and School Environment. New York University, 1969

342. Hamilton, Lorne D. The Issue of Public Aid to Catholic

Parochial Schools in the United States with Reference to Education in Quebec. Harvard University, 1953

343. Hancock, Greg. Public School, Parochial School: A Comparative Input-Output Analysis of Governmental and Catholic Elementary Schooling in a Large City. University of Chicago, 1971

344. Hartsell, Lee E. An Analysis of Judicial Decisions Regarding Academic Freedom in Public and Private Elementary and Secondary Schools and Institutions of Higher Education. Auburn University, 1977.

345. Hekman, Bruce A. A Study of the English Programs and Inservice Teacher Training Opportunities in Selected Private, Church-Related High Schools. University of Illinois at Urbana, 1971

346. Hendricks, Leon. An Analysis of State Statutes, Policies and Practices Related to Public Financing of Urban Non-Public Parochial Schools: Elementary and Secondary. Loyola University of Chicago, 1979

347. Henson, James P. The Creative Thinking Abilities of Elementary Students in Public and Parochial Schools. Indiana University, 1967.

348. Heron, William J. The Growth of Private Schools and Their Impact on the Public Schools of Alabama (1955-1975). University of Alabama, 1977

349. Hittner, Eunice. A Study of the Nature and Extent of Cooperation Between Public and Nonpublic Schools in Title III Pace Projects. The Catholic University of America, 1969

350. Holliday, Eileen F. Perceptions of Nonpublic Intermediate School Teachers Toward New Educational Approaches. University of Southern California, 1980.

351. Hume, Bonnie. Analysis of Two Current Arguments for Aid to Parochial Schools, University of Kentucky, 1964

352. Jabbour, Antoine G. The Interrelationships Among Size, Expenditure Level and Quality in Nonpublic Schools: The Case of the Seventh-Day Adventists Schools. The Catholic University of America, 1975

353. Johnson, John J. A Historical Analysis of Attempts to Secure Public Funds for Nonpublic Schools in the State of New Jersey. Rutgers University, 1978.

354. Jones, Robert D. An Analysis of Public Support of Private Schools. University of Southern California, 1958

355. Joyce, Bernita A. The Financial Viability of Private Elementary Schools: A Comparative Study. University of Santa Clara, 1974

356. Kaiser, M. Laurina (Sister). The Development of the Concept and Function of the Catholic Elementary School in the American Parish. Catholic University of America, 1955

357. Kalangis, George P. The Sociological and Religious Ethos of the Greek Parochial Schools in the American Southeast. Florida State University, 1979

358. Kizer, George A. An Analysis of the Drive for Public Funds for Parochial Schools, 1945-1963. University of Oklahoma, 1965

359. Kollap, Joseph B., Jr. Judicial Opinions Involving Public Funds or Services for Nonpublic Elementary and Secondary Schools. Duke University, 1974

360. Kurialacherry, Anthony J. The Financing of Private Education in Certain Democratic Countries. (A Comparative Study of the Systems in the U.S., Canada and India.) Loyola University of Chicago, 1962

361. LaBrake, John R. A Cooperative Public-Parochial Secondary School Venture: A Case Study. University of Maryland, 1977

362. Lackamp, Leo B. The Academic Achievement, Learning Interests, Self-Concept, Fate Control and Post High School Aspirations of Black Parochial and Public High School Students: A Comparative Study. University of Toledo, 1974

363. Lampre, Philip E. Comparative Study of the Assimilations of Mexican-Americans: Parochial Schools vs. Public Schools. Louisiana State University, 1973

364. Leary, Carolyn F. Perceived Goals and Characteristics of Jewish Day Schools and Catholic Parochial Schools. Fordham University, 1978

365. Lewis, Patricia M. N. A Study of the Financial Condition of Selected Private Independent Schools in the Commonwealth of Pennsylvania. University of Michigan, 1971

366. McCann, Donald F. Private and Public Secondary School Graduates: Their Articulation at the University of Denver. University of Denver, 1977

367. McCune, Richard D. A Study of the Composition and Design of School Boards in Selected Private and Parochial High Schools in California. University of Southern California, 1970

368. McDonnell, Thomas F. Private-Regarding Ideology and Its Relationship to Public Education: A Case Study. Pennsylvania State Universty, 1979

369. McGrew, Elliott, B., Jr. The Private School: A Study of American Phenonmenon. University of Minnesota, 1971

370. McKay, Richard K. Precarious Organizations: A Study of Maryland's Nonpublic Specialized Schools. The Johns Hopkins University, 1962

371. McLachlan, James S. The Education of the Rich: The Origin and Development of the Private Prep School, 1778-1916. Columbia University, 1966

372. Maltby, Gregory P. The Growth of Private Education: A Study of the Parents Attending an Episcopal Day School. University of Illinois at Urbana, 1966

373. Mathias, Kenneth W. An Historical and Status Survey of Member Schools of the Mississippi Private School Association from 1957 Until 1974. University of Mississippi, 1975

374. Melleky, John G. The Status of Parochial Elementary and Secondary Schools as Reflected by Selected Judicial Decisions Since 1925. University of Pittsburgh, 1964

375. Mercieca, Charles. An Investigation into the Applicability of Dewey's Methodology in All American Schools, Public and Private. University of Kansas, 1966

376. Molnar, Kathleen M. Nonpublic Schools and Neighborhood Stability: Geographic Considerations for Public Policy in Education. University of Minnesota, 1976

377. Mulligan, Robert T. The Status and Role of the Lay Tea-

cher in the Catholic Elementary Parochial School in the Nineteenth Century. The Catholic University of America, 1967

378. Murray, George F. A Study of Parental Opinion Toward Catholic Parochial Schools and Some Influential Factors. Boston University School of Education, 1959

379. Nash, Nicholas D. Forecasting the Future of Nonpublic School Policies: An Exploratory Study Using the Delphi Methodology. University of Minnesota, 1975

380. Nees, Dale R. A Case Study of Selected Changes in a Private School. University of California, Los Angeles, 1972

381. Novotney, Jerrold M. The Organizational Climate of Parochial Schools. University of California, Los Angeles, 1965

382. O'Breza, John E. Philadelphia Parochial School System from 1830-1920: Growth and Bureaucratization. Temple University, 1979

383. O'Connor, Frances R. College Preparatory Curricula in Nonpublic Schools: A Study and a Model. University of Massachusetts, 1974

384. Olson, Manley E. Use of Public Funds for Transporting Pupils Who Attend Nonpublic School. University of Minnesota, 1972

385. O'Neill, Patrick H. A Survey of Curriculum Offerings in Religious Education Programs in Catholic Private Secondary Schools of the Middle Atlantic States Association. The Catholic University of America, 1969

386. Page, William. Tort Liability of Private Schools and Charitable Institutions. Temple University, 1952

387. Powell, Theodore. Education, Religion and Politics: A Study of the Contemporary Conflict Over Public Services for Parochial School Pupils in Connecticut. Columbia University, 1958

388. Price, Bruce K. A Study of the Opinions of Educational, Civic and Religious Leaders Concerning the Feasibility of Providing State Financial Aid for Nonpublic Education in Maryland. The American University, 1973

389. Radloff, John P. Public School Transportation in the United States: The Legal Status of Transporting Parochial Pupils and the

Utilization of Transportation to Achieve Racial Balance.   University
of Denver, 1969.

390.   Rangel, Robert E.   Perceptions of Public School Teachers
in an ESEA Title I, Nonpublic School Program.   University of Southern California, 1979

391.   Rarig, Kathleen G.   Parental Reasons for Enrolling Children in a Private School in 1979 as Compared to Their Reasons in
1974.   Rutgers University, 1980

392.   Reed, Charles E.   An Analysis of the Perceptions of the
High School Principals in Public and Parochial Schools Relative to
the Importance of Sex Education in the Curriculum.   Southern Illinois
University at Carbondale, 1971

393.   Riggott, Stephen T.   The Relationship Between Selected Parochial School Teacher Characteristics and Attitudes Toward Gifted Elementary School Children.   The Catholic University of America, 1980

394.   Riley, Maureen E.   Female Non-Stereotyping in Parochial
and Public High Schools: An Analysis of Catholic Students' Attitudes
and Their Literary Preferences.   Boston University, 1978

395.   Rivell, Gerard J.   Aid to Private Schools and the 'Child
Benefit' Theory--A Historical Study of the Legal Impact of Two Key
Supreme Court Decisions.   Boston University, 1972

396.   Rutter, Michael T.   Educaid--A Rationale and a Model for
Granting Financial Aid to the Nonpublic School Students in Michigan.
Michigan State University, 1969

397.   Sabatino, Robert A.   Parental Perceptions of the Public
School: A Comparison of Parochial School Parents' Perceptions with
Those of Public School Parents.   Ohio State University, 1970

398.   Sansing, James A.   A Descriptive Survey of Mississippi's
Private, Segregated Elementary and Secondary Schools in 1971.   Mississippi State University, 1971

399.   Santee, Jack W.   Litigation Involving the Contractual Agree-
ments of Private Schools with Teachers, Parents and Students.   Miami
University, 1975

400.   Schultz, Richard H.   A Survey of Nonpublic High Schools of
North Carolina.   Duke University, 1969

401.   Shanahan, Patrick E.   State Laws Providing for the Transportation of Nonpublic School Children: Their Nature, Interpretation and Execution.   The Catholic University of America, 1960

402.   Shuda, Robert L.   Attitudes on State Aid to Nonpublic Education: A Case Study of Michigan Legislators.   University of Chicago, 1971

403.   Shulman, Bernhard H.   A Study of the Relationship of Parent Known Fact Information and Parent Expressed Private Opinion of an Innovative School Program.   Boston College, 1970

404.   Sikkenga, Roger W.   A Developmental Model for Broadly Representative State Organizations of Private Schools.   Florida Atlantic University, 1980

405.   Smith, Basil A.   The Legal Status of the Private Schools as Determined by Court Decisions.   University of Southern California, 1950

406.   Stellitano, John B.   An Exploration of Citizens' Awareness of the Shared Time Concept and Their Orientation Toward Private and Public School Collaboration.   Boston University, 1974

407.   Sullivan, Daniel J.   An Analysis of Public Aid to Existing Nonpublic Schools.   Yale University, 1974

408.   Sullivan, Harold J.   "De Facto" School Segregation: Private Choice or Public Policy?   City University of New York, 1978

409.   Taddie, John A.   A Comparison of the Academic Achievements of Mennonite Pupils Attending Mennonite Parochial Schools and Public Schools in Lancaster County, Pennsylvania.   Lehigh University, 1970

410.   Tave, Susan D.   An Evaluation of Alternative Modes of Citizen Participation in Public, Private and Parochial School Systems.   University of Michigan, 1973

411.   Trost, Albert R.   A Comparison of Public and Parochial Elementary Schools as Agents of Political Socialization.   Washington University, 1971

412.   Tullis, Rex L.   A Model for the Establishment of a Private Elementary School for a Church of the Nazarene.   Ball State University, 1979

413.   Twomley, Dale E.   An Analysis of Federal and State Supreme Court Cases on Financial Aid to Nonpublic Elementary and Secondary Education.   University of Maryland, 1977

414.   Voss, Elizabeth M.   A Descriptive-Comparative Study of Selected Values of Students from a Private Elementary School and Students from the Public Schools.   University of Northern Colorado, 1973

415.   Watters, John A.   The Effect of Nonpublic School Enrollment in Grades I-VI, on Per Pupil Expenditures in Connecticut School Districts.   University of Connecticut, 1964

416.   Weisblatt, Donna L.   A Study of the Bases for Parents' Choice of a Nonpublic Elementary School for Their Child.   Case Western Reserve University, 1976

417.   Wheeler, Ethel M.   How "Montessorian" Are the Montessori Schools?   A Study of Selected Montessori Schools with Respect to Their Adherence to the Montessori Tradition.   Rutgers University, 1975

418.   Will, Robert F.   An Analysis of the Legal Responsibilities of State Departments of Education for Nonpublic Schools.   University of Maryland, 1958

419.   Williams, John B., III.   Desegregating Private Secondary Schools: A Southern Example.   Harvard University, 1977

420.   Yates, Donald C.   Home and School Relations: The Private Tutor and the School.   Columbia University Teachers College, 1980

421.   Zimmerman, Florence A.   A Study of the Relationship Between Health Factors and Academic Performance of the Child in Urban Parochial Elementary Schools.   Temple University, 1980

APPENDIX

NATIONAL AND STATE ASSOCIATIONS

Alternative Schools Network. Jack Wuest, Head. 1105 West Lawrence Street, Chicago IL 60640.

Alumni Presidents' Council of Independent Secondary Schools. Mrs. J. Howard Marshall, President. 1189 Washington Street, Gloucester MA 01930.

American Association for Gifted Children. Anne E. Impellizzeri, President. 15 Gramercy Park, New York NY 10003.

American Lutheran Education Association. Donald A. Vetter, Executive Director. Wartburg College, Waverly IA 59677.

American Montessori Society. Bretta Weiss, Director. 159 Fifth Avenue, Suite 293, New York NY 19911.

Association of Evangelical Lutheran Churches--Education Division. F. Carl Kretzmann, Director. 3212 Ryan Avenue, Philadelphia PA 19136.

Association of Independent Colleges and Schools. Stephen B. Friedheim, President. 1730 M Street, N.W., Washington D.C. 20036.

Association of Independent Maryland Schools. Mrs. Blair D. Stambaugh, President. P.O. Box 21146, Severna Park MD 21146.

Association of Lutheran Secondary Schools. Herbert C. Moldenhauser, President. 16259 Nine Mile Road, East Detroit MI 48021

Association of Military Colleges and Schools of the U.S. W.C. Atkinson, President. P.O. Box 1309, Alexandria VA 22313

Association of Seventh-Day Adventist Educators. Richard T. Orrison, President. Andrews University, Berrien Springs MI 49104.

Association of Southern Baptist Colleges and Schools. Arthur L. Walker, Jr., Executive Director. 460 James Robertson Parkway, Nashville TN 37219.

Association of Teachers in Independent Schools of New York City and Vicinity. Ira Kochenthal, Executive Secretary. 1239 Park Avenue, New York NY 10028.

Christian Schools International. Michael T. Ruiter, Executive Director. 3350 East Paris Avenue, S.E., Grand Rapids MI 49508.

Connecticut Association of Independent Schools. A. William Olsen, Jr., President. Box 1310, Madison CT 06443

Council for American Private Education. Robert L. Smith, Executive Director. 1625 Eye Street, Suite 1010, Washington D.C. 20006.

Council for Religion in Independent Schools. Robert A. Moss, Director. 107 South Broad Street, Kenneth Square PA 19348.

Country Day School Headmasters' Association. Richard M. Garten, President. Princeton Day School, P.O. Box 75, The Great Road, Princeton NJ 08540.

Florida Council of Independent Schools. Edgar T. McCleary, Executive Secretary. 4227 West Kennedy Boulevard, Tampa FL 33609.

Friends Council on Education. Adelbert Mason, Executive Director. 1597 Cherry Street, Philadelphia PA 19102.

Georgia Association of Independent Schools, Inc. Fred H. Loveday, Executive Secretary. 3209 Isoline Way, Smyrna GA 30080.-

Headmasters Association. James H. M. Quinn, President. Harvard School, 3700 Coldwater Canyon Road, North Hollywood CA 9160.

Independent Schools Association of Northern New England. Richard L. Goldsmith, Executive Secretary. R.F.D. One, Bridgton ME 04009.

Independent Schools Association of the Central States. James Henderson, Jr., President. 1400 West Maple Avenue, Downers Grove IL 60515.

Independent Schools Association of the Southwest, Inc. Richard W. Ekdahl, Executive Director. P.O. Box 52297, Tulsa OK 74152.

Jesuit Secondary Education Association. Helen Dych, Executive Secretary. 1717 Massachusetts Avenue, N.W., Washington DC 20036.

Jewish Teachers Association. Michael Leinwand, President. 45

East 33rd Street, New York NY 10016.

Lutheran Church-Missouri Synod.   Board of Parish Education.   35-38 South Jefferson Avenue, St. Louis MO 63118.

Lutheran Education Association.   W. James Kirchoff, Head.   7400 Augusta Boulevard, River Forest IL 60305.

Maine Association of Independent Schools.   Arthur A. Dexter, President.   Lincoln Academy, Newcastle ME 04553.

Mid-South Association of Independent Schools.   J. Russell Frank, Executive Secretary.   1577 Chateau Drive, Atlanta GA 39328.

National Association of Christian Schools.   M. Van Schuyver, Executive Secretary.   Box 550, Wheaton IL 60187.

National Association of Hebrew Day School PTA's.   Mrs. Samuel Brand, Executive Secretary.   229 Park Avenue South, New York NY 10003.

National Association of Episcopal Schools, Inc.   Susie Bennett, Executive Coordinator.   815 Second Avenue, New York NY 10017.

National Association of Independent Schools.   Mr. John C. Esty, Jr., Director.   18 Tremont Street, Boston MA 02108.

National Association of Principals of Schools for Girls.   Constance B. Pratt, Executive Secretary.   910 Lathrop Street, Stanford CA 94305.

National Association of Private, Nontraditional Schools and Colleges. H. Earl Heusser, Executive Director.   1129 Colorado Avenue, Suite 320, Grand Junction CO 81501.

National Association of Private Schools for Exceptional Children. Dr. Sally Sibley, Director.   7201 Wimsatt Road, Springfield VA 22151.

National Association of Schools and Colleges of the United Methodist Church.   James S. Barrett, Executive Secretary.   P.O. Box 871, Nashville TN 37202.

National Catholic Educational Association.   Rt. Rev. Msgr. John F. Meyers, President.   One Dupont Circle, Suite 350, Washington D.C. 20036.

National Education Council of the Christian Brothers. Brother Francis Huether, Executive Secretary. 100 De LaSalle Road, Lockport IL 60441.

National Union of Christian Schools. Michael T. Ruiter, Executive Director. 865 28th Street, S.E., Grand Rapids MI 49508.

New Jersey Association of Independent Schools. Cintra S. Rodgers, Executive Secretary. 42 Norwood Avenue, Summit NJ 07901.

New York State Association of Independent Schools. Stephen Hinrichs Executive Director. 33 Warder Drive, Pittsford NY 14534.

New York State Council of Catholic School Superintendents. J. Alan Davitt, Executive Secretary. 11 North Pearl Street, Albany NY 1220

North Carolina Association of Independent Schools. Joseph M. Lalley, Jr., Chairman. St. Genevieve's/Gibbons Hall School, 103 Victoria Road, Asheville NC 28801.

Pennsylvania Association of Private Academic Schools, Inc. Mrs. John Savage, Executive Secretary. P.O. Box 571, Bryn Mawr PA 19010.

Seventh-Day Adventist Board of Education, K-12. Fred S. Stephan, Executive Secretary. 6840 Eastern Avenue, N.W., Washington D.C. 20012.

Southern Association of Independent Schools. Morris C. Johnson, Executive Director. 100 Woodlawn Drive, N.E., Marietta GA 30067.

Torah Umesorah-National Society for Hebrew Day Schools. Rabbi Bernard Goldenberg, Chairman. 229 Park Avenue South, New York NY 10003.

United States Catholic Conference. Department of Education. Rev. Thomas G. Gallagher, Secretary. 1312 Massachusetts Avenue, N.W., Washington D.C. 20005.

United Synagogue Commission on Jewish Education. Rabbi Joel H. Zaiman, Chairman. 155 Fifth Avenue, New York NY 10010.

Vermont Headmasters' Association, Inc. Richard H. Breen, Executive Secretary. P.O. Box 310, Northfield VT 05663.

Virginia Association of Independent Schools. Mrs. Jack N. Herod,

Executive Secretary.   711 St. Christopher's Road, Richmond VA 23226.

Virginia Association of Independent Special Education Facilities. Joanne Dondero, Executive Secretary.   7291 Wilmsatt Road, Springfield VA 22151

SUBJECT INDEX

AUTHOR INDEX